The High-Pressure Steam Engine Investigated: An Exposition of Its Comparative Merits, and an Essay Towards an Improved System of Construction, Adapted Especially to Secure Safety and Economy in Its Use

Ernst Alban

THE

HIGH-PRESSURE STEAM ENGINE

INVESTIGATED.

.

₊ *This Translation was commenced in the early part of 1845, and a great portion of the following pages has been in type more than twelve months; but the numerous engagements of the Translator having presented obstacles to the completion of his task, it has been deemed advisable to publish the First and Second Parts without further delay. The Third and Fourth Parts, illustrated with Plates, will be published in the months of March and June in the present year.*

PRINTED BY W. HUGHES,
KING'S HEAD COURT, GOUGH SQUARE.

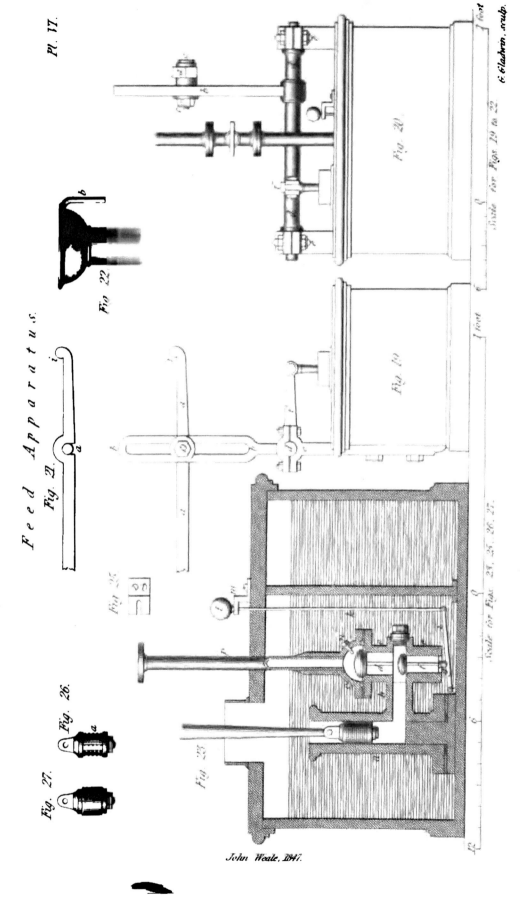

Feed Apparatus.

Pl. VI.

Fig. 21.

Fig. 22.

Fig. 26.

Fig. 27.

Fig. 23.

Fig. 19.

Fig. 20.

John Weale, 1847.

THE

HIGH-PRESSURE STEAM ENGINE

INVESTIGATED:

AN EXPOSITION OF ITS COMPARATIVE MERITS,

AND

AN ESSAY TOWARDS AN IMPROVED SYSTEM OF CONSTRUCTION,

ADAPTED ESPECIALLY TO SECURE SAFETY AND ECONOMY IN ITS USE.

BY DR. ERNST ALBAN,

PRACTICAL MACHINE MAKER, PLAU, SAXONY.

Translated from the German, with Notes,

BY WILLIAM POLE, F.R.A.S.,

ASSOCIATE OF THE INSTITUTION OF CIVIL ENGINEERS;
PROFESSOR OF ENGINEERING IN ELPHINSTONE COLLEGE, BOMBAY;
AND LECTURER ON ASTRONOMY AND STEAM MACHINERY TO THE INDIAN NAVY.

PARTS I. AND II.

WITH SIX PLATES, ENGRAVED BY MR. GLADWIN.

London:
JOHN WEALE, 59, HIGH HOLBORN.
M.DCCC.XLVII.

ADVERTISEMENT.

IT is possible that the first impression of the English reader on perusing the title-page of this work, may be that of surprise at being referred to the writings of a foreigner, and to the results of foreign experience, for information on a subject so essentially English as that of the Steam Engine. England is, it will be said, not only the birth-place of this machine, but the country in which it has gained all the progressive developement that has fitted it for its present magnificent sphere of usefulness;—the English have been the inventors and improvers, and are *par excellence* the manufacturers of the Steam Engine;—and, it may be asked, is it consistent with our national honour to be sent to another country for information on a subject allowed, almost by common consent, to be peculiarly and exclusively our own?

This inquiry is natural enough, but it has a very simple and satisfactory answer. The Steam Engine is not a machine whose principles of construction and action are invariable: it admits of many modifications; or rather we should say the properties of steam may be made use of by many diversified methods to obtain the desired result,—the production of mechanical power; and therefore if it can be shown that any one of these, which offers the prospect of advantage in its application, have been neglected by ourselves as a nation, we need not be surprised if our neighbours should step in before us upon the untrodden path, nor in such case need we be ashamed of receiving instruction from them, as they have been accustomed to receive it, but in a much greater measure, from us heretofore.

Now it cannot be denied that ever since the time of New-comen, the attention of the English has been almost exclusively directed to that modification of the Steam Engine which depends for its source of power principally upon the *condensibility* of steam, namely, the *low-pressure condensing engine*, in which a very moderate elasticity is used. The other great class, comprising that variety of engine which owes its efficiency principally to the *elasticity* of the steam,—the HIGH-PRESSURE ENGINE,—is (or at least was a very few years ago) scarcely known among us in comparison. While we find the condensing engine studied carefully, treated of most voluminously, and manufactured by wholesale, we deplore the neglect which the high-pressure engine has suffered;—we look in vain for information upon it; and we are scarcely able to point, even in the present more cultivated field of locomotives, to a solitary specimen deserving the name of an economical producer of steam power. Surely then, while we have done so little with this variety of the machine, we need not scruple to attend to the investigations, and to profit by the experience, of those who have done more; and it is on this ground we invite attention to the following pages.

It must startle English Engineers not a little to be told that the high-pressure engine is both safer and more economical in its use than the low-pressure condensing one; yet such is the declaration of our Author, who, according to his own showing, appears to have devoted more attention to the high-pressure engine than perhaps any other Engineer now in practice. On this account, if for no other, the work we now lay before the public is worthy of a careful and impartial examination.

The claim the Author puts forward to consideration as an

authority on the matter he treats of, may be gathered from the following extract from his Preface. He says, "For the course of now about thirty years have I uninterruptedly laboured in the field of knowledge offered by the steam engine, and for the far greater part of that time my attention has been directed to the high-pressure variety. I have erected a considerable number of engines of this description, of various sizes, and from all these I have gained opportunities of gradually carrying out into actual practice the results of my experiments and observations. I have also had the advantage of a two years' residence in England, where the opportunity was afforded me of observing and experimenting upon hundreds of steam engines, of the most diversified kinds, and applied to the greatest variety of purposes: and more than all I have found by experience that my endeavours to accomplish the improvement of the high-pressure engine have had a constantly increasing success. On these grounds I have reason to hope that I may not be considered incompetent to the task I have undertaken, and that my statements and reasonings may be received with confidence."

But these grounds for such an estimation of the Author's qualifications for his work are scarcely necessary; the book itself furnishes ample internal evidence in its own favour. We are at no loss to discover that the Author has had much practical acquaintance with his subject;—that he has improved to the utmost advantage all the opportunities of observation and investigation which his practice has afforded him;—that he has taken much pains to make himself master of whatever has been previously done or written by others; and that he has brought to bear on his task a sound practical judgment, an acute and comprehensive habit of observation, a close and forcible method of reasoning, and above all a candid and unbiassed mind, anxious to discover the truth, and never ashamed to confess a past error, or to change a previously expressed opinion, when such a course has been dictated to him by the results of future experience and investigation. The ample and copious discussion given to every point of importance upon which difference of opinion has been found to exist, or which has been complicated in its nature and difficult of decision, and the honest endeavour to present impartially the whole view of both sides of a disputed question, testify not only the extent of the Author's information, but the careful and impartial manner in which he has endeavoured to deduce a correct conclusion from the knowledge he has gained, and his evident anxiety to put his readers in full possession of the reasons which have guided him to his decision.

The First Part of the work, it will be perceived, treats of the High-pressure Engine generally. After a few articles of introductory matter, the Author proceeds, *first*, to examine the principal objections brought against the high-pressure engine, dwelling more particularly on that one which has proved the greatest obstacle hitherto to its more general use; namely, its alleged danger. The various causes which tend to produce explosions of steam engine boilers are discussed at length, and proof produced, both from reasoning and from experience, that low-pressure boilers are not less liable to such destructive accidents than high-pressure, if only proper care is used in the construction of the latter. The errors often committed in the manufacture of vessels for the generation of high-pressure steam are pointed out, and many excellent remarks and considerations in regard to boiler and furnace arrangements in general will be found under this head. After noticing other objections as to economy, &c., the Author proceeds, *secondly*, to show the peculiar advantages possessed by the high-pressure engine; as simplicity, compactness, cheapness, lightness, conveniences of various kinds in working, and particularly economy of fuel.

The SECOND PART treats in detail of the Boiler and its Appurtenances, and the Furnace; the THIRD PART will be devoted to the Engine itself; and the FOURTH PART will contain some examples of its application to various purposes: these will be illustrated by plates, and will contain the developement of the views to which the Author has been led as to the methods of construction best adapted to secure the ends proposed, namely, safety and economy in the use of the high-pressure engine.

I have only a word or two to add as to my share in the present publication. The translation of a work of this kind, whose object is to convey technical information, ought, I conceive, to be undertaken in a somewhat different manner from that of writings whose principal value lies in their literary merit. In the latter the rendering must be as close as the nature of the two languages will permit, or the work becomes in fact more the Translator's than the Author's: but with the former, where the purpose is to present correctly the *matter* of the book independently of the *manner*, the object of the Translator must be to seize upon the ideas intended to be conveyed, and to put them in such a dress as will be most adapted to the technical character and language of the subject treated of, without much regard to the style of phraseology of the original. In my endeavour to accomplish this, I have not hesitated to take occasionally some liberties in the translation, sometimes departing widely from the literal rendering, but always keeping in view the more perfect adaptation of the Author's meaning to the ideas and language of English engineering science. . I have used my own discretion in omitting here and there such matter as seemed to me wanting in novelty or connection with the subject, and, (though with a more sparing hand,) I have here and there added something which I conceived might make the Author's meaning more clear, or his reasoning more conclusive. The original is enriched with a great number of references; but as these are mostly to foreign works, I have omitted the greater part, believing them to be but of little use to the English reader. I have, I think, somewhat improved the *arrangement* of the work, by dividing off the matter in a more systematic manner than the Author has done, and by numbering the Articles. I have also added a synoptical *Table of Contents*, which presents at one view a general idea of the subject matter of the Treatise, and by means of which, reference to any particular item is rendered more easy.

Should any slight verbal irregularities appear in the translation, (and many know how difficult it is to prevent such from creeping in when writing from a foreign language,) my apology must be that I have been unable, for obvious reasons, to pass the proof sheets under my own eye for revision.

WILLIAM POLE.

Bombay, August, 1845.

CONTENTS.

PART I.

PAGE

INTRODUCTION.

ON THE HIGH-PRESSURE ENGINE GENERALLY.

EXAMINATION OF THE PRINCIPAL OBJECTIONS BROUGHT AGAINST THE HIGH-PRESSURE ENGINE.

PART II.

ON THE BOILER AND ITS APPENDAGES: AND THE FURNACE.

THE BOILER.

INTRODUCTION.

1. IT would be superfluous here to attempt to enumerate the benefits which the steam engine has conferred upon mankind. It is matter of universal knowledge that all branches of industry have, since its introduction into use, made most important advances through its aid; and every day's experience shows it constantly extending its beneficial influence to new and important purposes, and lending its powerful assistance to the further advance of civilization. When we consider what the introduction of the steam engine has already done, we have the less difficulty in anticipating that this invention may yet be destined to achieve objects of whose magnitude and importance we can at present form but a faint idea.

2. On this account, it is greatly to be wondered at that such a noble invention has not been brought to a higher grade of perfection. When it is considered what multitudes of labourers have been working in the field of its improvement;—what variety of points in the system the improvers have directed their attention to;—what manifold opinions have been advanced;—and how many thousand means have been tried to gain the desired end;—it must

A

appear astounding that all these efforts have produced
so little real knowledge with respect to the great de-
sideratum,—the most suitable and appropriate means of
employing steam as a moving power,—and have left the
question, at what point to commence improvement in
order to arrive at the greatest degree of perfection, still
undecided.

3. Yet more inexplicable, however, is the fact, that
among all that has been done, we find such a want of
experimental information as to the comparative value of
the different known modifications of the machine by
which the power of steam is made available ; so few comparative experiments conducted in a scientific and impartial manner, which might tend to award to one system
or another its relative degree of superiority, and so to lead
to a determinate conclusion respecting this important
element of the problem.

Up to the present time we find only a few scattered
experiments undertaken by isolated individuals or by industrial associations; but this little does not suffice, and
we can only hope to arrive fully at the wished-for object
when the question is made a national one, and when a
national purse will be available in order to secure a set
of investigations, of proper extent, and made with a
degree of care, leisure, and philosophical knowledge, com-
mensurate with the importance of the design.   The
labours of those isolated individuals who have given their
attention to the subject, have been frequently restricted
to theoretical reasonings and calculations, which, often
being biassed by prejudice, party spirit, or egotism, or as
frequently proceeding from untenable hypotheses, have

not only failed in the desired object, but have tended yet further to increase the range of existing error: and when the labours of such have been of an experimental kind, they have generally had too limited a character, and have stood too wide apart, to throw much light upon the matter, or lead to any satisfactory general conclusions. Isolated individuals are seldom possessed of the proper means for the perfect attainment of their well-intentioned ends; while those who have the best opportunities and capabilities for the work, are usually withheld by the want of leisure, or other adverse circumstances, from prosecuting to a successful result the designs they might otherwise willingly undertake. The machine maker, careful for the most part after his own pecuniary advantage and the interests of his trade, frequently sacrifices to these objects the cause of science: the simplification of machinery tends to lessen the amount of his work and to diminish the number of its admirers, inasmuch as complicated looking machines more readily attract the attention of the purchaser than those of a more simple and less imposing appearance.[1] Moreover, the search

---

[1] This remark may probably be just in more cases than it is unjust; but we have among our British manufacturing engineers many brilliant exceptions. The mere mention of the names of Maudslay and Field, Rennie, Miller, Fairbairn, and others of similar character, would show that the spirit of investigation is not always damped by such considerations as those mentioned in the text. The following extract from 'A Treatise on the Cornish Engine,' by the translator of this work, bears closely on the point insisted on.—Tr.

"It is necessary to say something of the relations which subsist between the mining adventurer, the engineer, and the manufacturer of machinery in Cornwall, as their respective positions are somewhat peculiar, and different to those which obtain in the rest of the kingdom; and to this peculiarity may be traced much of the opportunity of improvement which has been afforded.

"In London and in the country generally, parties who require steam engines after truth is beset with so many difficulties, and yet oftentimes the discovery, when made, appears so simple and of so little merit, as to offer but small inducement to

are accustomed to apply for them directly to the manufacturers, who thus become the *designers* as well as the makers of the engines; or if a civil engineer intervene, it is usually only to the general arrangement of the works that he directs his attention, leaving the details of the construction of the engine to the manufacturer, as before. The *management* of the engine, when erected, is intrusted (except in the cases of large works where a managing engineer is specially engaged) generally to the engine-man, or to parties having but little claim to the acquirements necessary for its skilful and economical performance.

" But in Cornwall things are otherwise arranged. There is a class of men, known by the name of *engineers*, who have no connection at all with the manufacturers, and whose sole and proper occupation it is to take charge of the steam engines upon the mines, and to design and superintend the manufacture of new ones, when such are required. The manufacturers do not pretend to be engineers, and would on no account undertake to supply engines,* except through the intervention and under the direction of some of the engineers.

" Thus every mine has its engineer, who has absolute command over the management of the engine upon the works, and to whom the credit or discredit which may arise from the working of the engine consequently belongs. If alterations or new engines are called for, the designs are made by the engineer of the mine, who procures estimates of them from the manufacturer, and superintends the due execution of the works.

" The advantages arising from this separation of the offices of the engineer and manufacturer are too important to be overlooked.

" A manufacturer has generally too much to attend to in the arrangements of his workshop to be able to devote much time to consider the improvement and watch the working of the engines he makes; and the matters which of necessity engage his daily attention are generally of too pressing and harassing a nature to allow of much study being given to the principles of what he is doing. Hence (although we know there are many honourable exceptions to this rule) we find that too frequently manufacturers are content to imitate the examples of those who have preceded them, and that what alterations are

---

* *I. e.* for the mining districts: it is not uncommon for the manufacturers to undertake contracts on their own responsibility for other parts of the kingdom, or for abroad.

those who would seek for themselves; while in occasional instances the impediments of party feeling, a fear to deviate from the beaten track, or a bigoted attachment to some favourite principle in fashion at the time, all tend to discourage the hope of a speedy attainment of the desirable end by private and isolated endeavours.

Notwithstanding these discouragements, however, it is yet the bounden duty of all individuals to record and publish what they are able to contribute to the general stock of information, as by so doing they will at any rate furnish a collection of facts which may be of essential service in future investigations.

4. No one will dispute that heretofore too little has been done with the High-pressure Engine to determine

made, are only such as are suggested by the necessity of the case, and adopted often without due consideration.

"But in Cornwall the *engineers* are able to devote their whole attention to the improvement of the engine, unharassed by the cares of the manufactory, and are ever alive to the consideration of all circumstances connected with its action which can influence its duty: they have opportunities of trying experiments with a view to improvement, which it would generally be impossible for a manufacturer to undertake; and when they find these successful, they have the power to extend their application and see the effect of their working.

"Another circumstance which is also very favourable to the execution of the plans of improvement projected by the engineer is, that models are not generally charged for by the manufacturers. The expense of patterns is often a great barrier to the progress of improvement, by enhancing the cost of experiments on a large scale; but in Cornwall this does not operate, for (unless in particular cases which form exceptions to the general rule) this expense is borne by the manufacturers, and the engineers are free to make what alterations or experiments they please, without any direct charge being made for the necessary models.

"There can be no doubt that to this state of things is owing much of the improvement which has been made in the Cornish engine;—more perhaps than to any other cause, with the exception of the introduction of the duty reports."

its true value and place among the range of varieties of
the steam engine. Its discussion, up to the present time,
has been mixed up with so many diversified opinions,
and replete with so much that is erroneous, unscientific,
and contradictory, that it has only served to perplex the
matter more and more, and to disgust the industrial com-
munity at large. The subject is beset with so many
wants,—is yet so loosely treated in its philosophical
bearings, and its practical application so imperfectly understood,—that experiments and researches of even the
most ordinary character need no apology for their publication.

The English have in a great measure assisted in bringing this form of engine into discredit, if not by open
attacks, yet through the bad construction and arrangement of their engines;[2] and it would have stood a chance
of again passing into oblivion, had not the French, at a
late date, bestirred themselves to prevent its downfall by
examining and making known its advantages, and by a
series of gradual improvements in its construction.
America and France remain the only supports of the
system; while in Germany but little interest has been
excited in its favour, and its defenders have been, in
Anglican fashion, openly opposed and condemned. The
high-pressure engine has generally been conceded only
a very limited field of application, and considered as
only applicable to a certain range of objects. The late
introduction of railways, and the great interest excited
by them in all quarters, seem, however, now about to
place the principle of the high-pressure engine in a

---

[2] This remark is a little tinged with the usual prejudice of the author against
England; but we must confess it is not altogether devoid of truth.—Tr.

higher point of view. It is generally found, that a subject which has lain for a time dormant, has on its revival been taken up with greater zeal than before; and thus it is we now find that in England, so long exclusively the country of the WATT engine, the high-pressure plan is occupying the attention of engineers, and furnishing employment for the workshops throughout the land. The locomotive engine is now the watchword; information on the subject rises in value, and improvements and alterations succeed each other with unwonted rapidity. Thus England appears again about to become the mart for the high-pressure engine, and all now look to that enlightened nation for the perfect dispersion of the obscurity in which the subject has heretofore been enveloped.

5. The principal object of this my work will be to make known a series of experiments and observations undertaken by me; partly on engines which I have constructed for various establishments, partly on two which have been working daily under my own eyes;—to specify the researches that have occupied me uninterruptedly for a long term of years, with their unsuccessful as well as their successful results;—and to exhibit the train of ideas in reference to the improvement of the machine, which I have deduced from the whole. My objects have been, in the first place, to lessen, or rather entirely to remove, the dangers supposed to attend the use of high-pressure steam; and, secondly, to discover a plan of construction on the simplest possible principles, which should always correspond with, and be adapted to, the work to be done by the engine. In order to make myself intelligible to

those classes who are not skilled in the higher branches
of physical and mathematical science, I have avoided as
much as possible all calculations of a complex nature and
of doubtful utility, especially such as are based on simple
hypotheses, and not upon positive truth. I well know
the danger of treading on such uncertain ground, and I
have therefore restricted myself to drawing simple conclusions from simple experiments, and to forming, from
these conclusions, simple rules for practice. If these do
not always bear the stamp of high mathematical rigour,
I dare assert that they are not of the less practical value,
for I have never known them to fail in the whole of my
experience as a manufacturer of high-pressure engines.
And who would presume, after all, to deduce leading rules
from theory in the present imperfect state of physical
knowledge as applied to the steam engine? Mathematics
can do nothing until a correct observation of nature paves
the way for its application; and of what use are pages
filled with algebraical formulæ, if after all we must, in
order to go securely, adapt our results to our circumstances, which comes, in fact, to nothing but working
ad libitum? While I have occupied myself with the
actual construction of steam engines, I have always
found, that if a sound judgment is brought to the task,
but little calculation is necessary in order to accomplish
a wished-for end. I have scarcely ever made engines
similar to each other, but all for different purposes; I
have had a manifold variety of circumstances to deal
with, and not unfrequently difficulties to overcome which
have led me out of the accustomed track; but I have
ever found myself able to attain the most desirable results
by the most simple means.

6. I hold it to be positively injudicious to recommend a certain form and construction of the high-pressure engine as an invariable standard. To a practised engine-maker a hundred different varieties ought to be at hand. He will, if he works wisely, strive to adapt these with practical skill to the purposes for which the engine is destined, and in all cases will endeavour to secure to the utmost extent the simplicity of the whole; for simplicity not only lessens the cost of construction, but makes the work more durable,—saves a considerable load of resistance,—increases the useful effect,—economizes fuel,—and tends to show to advantage the desirable properties of this kind of engine. Such an engineer will have the credit of stepping beyond the ordinary routine, and of elevating the profession of which he is a member.

I shall hereafter have occasion to show, that in order to attain the utmost simplicity, the general principles, as well as the details, of the high-pressure engine, may bear similar modifications without disadvantage; and I shall give designs of suitable arrangements for some of the most useful purposes to which steam engines are applied.[a]

---

[a] I have often been surprised to find how little attention is paid to this point in England. I have constantly seen there the most absurd combinations of engine and machinery: for example, one of the most common is that of working pumps by a rotatory engine. Here a rectilineal motion is first changed into a circular one, in order to be converted into a rectilineal one back again! In steam flour-mills we see engines at a distance from the machinery, and burdened with cumbersome fly-wheels, when by proper arrangements the momentum of the stones might render but small ones necessary, or in many cases might dispense with them altogether. Perhaps some of the English engineers adopt the vulgar error that a fly-wheel increases the power of the engine! But more of this hereafter.

[This allegation is, we must confess, but too true. When a manufacturer has made what is called "a set of patterns" for an engine, he is but too apt to make that form of engine serve for all possible sorts of purposes, without much attention to the propriety of the adaptation. This saves him expense, and gives him extra work in making the necessary connecting machinery. Some excuse may be found for using a rotatory engine for pumps, inasmuch as a steadiness of motion is thereby attained which it would be difficult to secure with small engines working rectilineally. With regard to the last paragraph of the note, we are sorry to add that the scientific and engineering literature of our country shows but too many instances where persons may be found to propagate and defend the doctrine of either gain or loss by the fly-wheel, or of loss by the crank or connecting-rod, or in short any other absurdity. Let us hope that the light of science is now so far spreading amongst us that these blots on our philosophical character may soon only be matters of history.—Tr.]

PART I.

ON THE HIGH-PRESSURE ENGINE GENERALLY.

7. IF we are to believe the accounts on record, that the first idea of the steam engine was suggested to the Marquis of Worcester by the blowing out of a cork from a flask of water which he had placed in too strong a heat, it is not easy to conceive how this accident could have led to the invention of engines working by condensation, which are mentioned in history as the first existing, and which Captain Savery brought into actual use. It seems much more probable that the result of the suggestion must have been a *high-pressure engine,* in the same manner as, at a later date, the bursting of a gun-barrel by steam, suggested to Oliver Evans the first idea of using high-pressure steam in his engines.

8. It is still more inexplicable that the high-pressure engine came so late into the field, and that nearly a whole century elapsed before this most simple method of applying the power of steam was brought prominently into notice.[1] The attention was confined almost ex-

---

[1] The explanation of this may probably be found in the fact, that it was so difficult in early days to make vessels and joints sufficiently strong to withstand

clusively to the production of a vacuum by condensation, in order to make use of the atmospheric pressure, or of steam of very low elasticity. A multitude of inventions have been called into being with reference to this plan, and it cannot be denied that great advances have been made in its improvement; so that the later built engines on this principle have become most perfect machines, and their application has in consequence been greatly extended. The names of a host of inventors have become illustrious in this field of discovery. The knowledge of the physics of steam has made much progress, and the general view of the subject has become much enlightened; yet no one, for so long a time, has dared to venture out of the beaten track, and to strike out for himself a new and successful path of exertion. To Oliver Evans was it reserved to show the true value of a long-known principle, and to establish thereon a new and more simple method of applying the power of steam; a method that will hereafter be greatly amplified, and will remain an eternal memorial to its introducer. The long delay of this revival affords a remarkable example of truths often shown by experience, namely, that the most plain and simple discoveries are generally reached through a labyrinth of complexities, and that even master minds are not free from the influence of habit and routine.

It is true that previously to the labours of Evans, Papin and Leupold had made use of high-pressure steam, and the latter proposed a real high-pressure engine in his *Theatrum Machinarum;* but the practical application

the high pressure. Savery, we know, experienced much inconvenience from this cause, and this it was indeed which principally prevented his engines from sustaining their ground.—Tr.

of the power was neglected, or at least we hear nothing more of the matter. Whether Oliver Evans was or was not aware of these suggestions is uncertain; but be this as it may, at all events he made the first actual high-pressure engine: his labours were crowned with success; and he showed clearly the great advantages to be derived from the plan. Indeed, to such perfection did he bring it, that Trevithick and Vivian, who came after him, followed but clumsily in his wake, and do not deserve the title of either inventors or improvers of the high-pressure engine, which the English are so anxious to award to them.[2] When it is considered under what unfavourable circumstances Oliver Evans worked, his merit must be much enhanced; and all the attempts made to lessen his fame, only show that he is neither understood nor equalled by his detractors.

9. The high-pressure engine is, however, in the present day, but little understood, and the great designs of its inventors but little appreciated: this is to be ascribed to the fact that its principles have never yet received the attention they deserve, although they have now been known forty years. Engines on this plan are treated as if already condemned: their advantages are generally doubted, or conceded only in a slight degree, and for certain applications; an outcry is made as to the great

[2] I give this as the author gives it, but not without protesting against the conclusion in the absence of proof in its favour. Unfortunately I am unable to procure data as to what Oliver Evans actually did, but the matter should be investigated, and I cordially recommend it to those able to take it up. Dr. Alban, when he mentions only Papin and Leupold, seems to forget that Savery's engines were, in the true sense of the word, *high-pressure* engines.—TR.

danger with which their use is attended; and some of the opponents of the system have even gone so far as to insist that legislative interference ought to be exercised to limit their use. Other objections are, that they are less economical in fuel, are more subject to wear and tear, and require more lubrication than low-pressure engines; with other evils of a similar character. That some of these charges are occasionally well founded, cannot be denied; but it can be shown that the machines are liable to them only when unskilfully made; and that when constructed on proper principles, they are not only as free from objection as low-pressure engines, but in many respects are much superior to them.

Now what are the defects which high-pressure engines have hitherto laboured under? How are these to be remedied in their future construction? and what principles must be followed in order to secure the manifold advantages which the system possesses? I will endeavour to answer these queries, as far as lies in my power, in the following pages; but previously I will give a closer examination of the objections brought against the use of the high-pressure engine. From such an examination will more naturally flow a developement of the principles which should be adopted in order to remove these objections, and to insure the advantages that may be obtained by a proper construction of the engine and a suitable application of the steam.

EXAMINATION OF THE PRINCIPAL OBJECTIONS BROUGHT AGAINST THE HIGH-PRESSURE ENGINE.

10. *First Objection.*—This is the danger alleged to attend its use. It is asserted that vessels wherein high-

pressure steam is generated and contained, must be more liable to burst than such as are used for low-pressure. This proposition seems intelligible and self-evident, and it attracts at first sight the attention of those who are unskilled in such matters; yet it is only true in a qualified sense. Before, however, I proceed to investigate it more closely, I will venture to appeal to experience for the best evidence as to its value, and to inquire whether high-pressure boilers have been found more liable to explosion than low-pressure.

11. No instances occur in the history of the steam engine where a destructive explosion has happened to the engine itself,[3] even those worked to the highest pressure. The steam cylinder, and valve-boxes, the only parts of the engine exposed to the action of the steam, have always been found, even with a small thickness of metal, secure and durable. This is to be ascribed to the circumstance that these vessels are not exposed to any destructive agency, except the friction of the piston and valves, and this being nearly harmless, they remain in a constant state of safety without deterioration. The boiler or steam generator of the engine is the only organ exposed to mischief, and with this alone destructive explosions are found to occur. Who then will assert that only high-pressure boilers are subject to danger, and that low-pressure ones are secure? Such an opinion would be at variance alike with theory and experience, for we may consider,—

[3] A late destructive accident with one of Messrs. Samuda's engines was of this nature, caused by the giving way of the steam-pipe at one of its joints. Such accidents are very rare.—Tr.

12. (*a.*) Every boiler may become supercharged with steam when the quantity drawn off is less than the quantity generated, and when the safety-valves, in consequence of imperfections in their action or condition, do not properly perform their duty. Therefore, in so far as similar safety apparatus are used for both high and low-pressure boilers, they must be liable to similar interruptions in their working. Experience has shown this very often, and it has been found that even the vertical open-mouthed feed-pipes of low-pressure boilers, which act as escape-pipes when the boiler pressure is too great, (these are wanting in marine engines,) are not always secure.[4] If then an overfilling of the boiler with steam is equally possible in both high and low-pressure engines, both are liable to danger from this source; as the strength of the metal is adapted to the working pressure, and therefore the proper elasticity for which the vessel is constructed must be exceeded when such an occurrence happens. But there is an advantage on the side of the high-pressure engine, for the elasticity must be increased in a much higher ratio than with the low-pressure engine, before it overcomes the pressure at which the boiler is proved (usually three times the working elasticity); and therefore a much longer time will elapse before absolute danger arises. For example, in a boiler working at eight atmospheres, it will take a much greater lapse of time for the pressure to rise to twenty-four atmospheres, than it would to reach 12 lbs. per square inch in a boiler working at 4 lbs.; and these would be the points at which danger may be supposed

---

[4] Vide Dingler's 'Polytechnische Journal,' vol. xv. page 142.

to arise in the respective cases.[5] This gives a key to the experience of late times, that as great a proportionate number of low as of high-pressure boilers have exploded, as well in England as in America and France; and that among the latest instances, the accidents with the former have reached an alarming extent.

13. (*b.*) All boilers alike become gradually deteriorated by the working of destructive agencies upon them, particularly through the constant action of the fire without and the water within; so that the thickness of the metal may become gradually diminished, and at last reach a point at which danger may arrive. The worst of this evil is that the progress of the deterioration cannot be properly estimated, in consequence of many unfavourable circumstances that often happen, without either the knowledge or the fault of the person who has charge of the machine, and which are variable in the amount of their action, being more injurious at one time than at another. Such may be the following:

(1.) The overheating of certain parts of the boiler by the water standing at too low a level. Upon these places the metal, especially if iron, becomes speedily oxidized,[6] this effect taking place on both sides, from the action of the fire on the outside and of the water

---

[5] M. Arago notices this in the 'Echo du Monde savant,' No. 484. He characterizes the fear of high-pressure boilers as mere prejudice.

[6] Iron, long exposed to the action of fire, loses its fibrous texture, and becomes brittle and crystalline. Löwe found that wrought iron, long exposed at a red heat to steam, became crystalline, and that even the heat alone produced this effect without the application of moisture. It is not easy to find the cause of this phenomenon in any chemical property of iron; but be it what it may, the fact is undoubted, and results in a weakening of the tenacity and cohesive force of the metal.

in the inside, the latter arising from the decomposition of the steam by the incandescent iron, and the consequent attraction of the oxygen to the metal.

(2.) Too great an accumulation, either general or partial, of scale or earthy sediment in the boiler. These substances being bad conductors of heat, prevent, when in large quantities, the proper distribution of caloric to the water, or at least injuriously retard its transmission. The heat of the metal then increases to too great an extent, and may frequently rise to incandescence. Sometimes it happens that the layers of deposit arrange themselves in such wise as to leave interstices to which the water cannot penetrate : now if any of the adjacent portions become cracked, the water will suddenly find its way upon the hot metal, and will cause a local explosion, thereby loosening the scale not only from the part previously affected, but for a considerable distance round, and consequently increasing the contact of the water with the heated metal. This produces a rumbling commotion in the water, which, if the incandescent spot be large, may be in the highest degree injurious to the structure of the boiler. The steam thus suddenly formed augments the pressure, and hence again increased danger may ensue, particularly as the spot overheated will have been rendered more susceptible of damage. It has often been remarked that explosions were immediately preceded by the rumbling noise alluded to above. The high-pressure engine has in this respect also an advantage over the low-pressure, in that the sediment, when the elasticity is great, seldom attaches itself firmly to the sides of the boiler, but collects in a loose state, and is easily removed.

(3.) Damage to the boiler-plate by careless cleaning. Whoever has watched the process of cleaning ordinary boilers, and observed the forcible knocking, hammering, and chiselling of the foul plates;—whoever has re-marked, to what ignorant and awkward men this work is intrusted, often without any superintendence;—and considers how the plates, perhaps already damaged by the fire, must in addition suffer from such violent handling;—will bear me out when I assign this process as frequently one of the principal causes of a speedy destruction of the boiler.

(4.) An unequal expansion between the several parts of the boiler, whereby damage often occurs, especially at the angles of the vessel. Those boilers which are constructed with fire-tubes or flues running through them are more especially exposed to this danger. Such tubes usually lie but a short depth below the water level, and therefore if the water falls short they soon become more heated than the external case of the boiler, and by the consequent greater degree of expansion, an injurious straining of the joints must necessarily ensue. The rents have been usually found at these joints when boilers of such a make have exploded.

But experience shows how little these destructive agencies have been heretofore attended to or remarked even by skilful parties; and we learn how difficult it is to discover their action or progress even when the attention is specially directed to them. We have instances where boilers have exploded immediately after examination, such as that of the American steam boat *Ætna*, and others of both high and low pressure.

14. (*c.*) Referring again to the possible accident of the falling of the water below its proper level, and the consequent incandescence of some part of the iron, we may remark that this heated portion of metal will, if at a sufficiently high temperature, generate hydrogen gas by the decomposition of the watery vapour. Hydrogen so produced has been long supposed to play an important part in steam boiler accidents, as it is conjectured it may inflame and explode inside the boiler. However, it must be recollected, that in order to produce this effect, the entrance of atmospheric air is absolutely necessary, and it is very difficult to conceive how air can enter in such quantity as to form an explosive compound with a large volume of hydrogen. The amount of air which may enter with the feed water is too insignificant to be taken into consideration, and an entrance of air through the usual safety-valves and openings of the boiler is only possible with low-pressure engines, but impossible with high-pressure ones for obvious reasons. With the former it may frequently happen, that during the working of the engine the pressure may sink below that of the atmosphere, and in this case air would easily enter,[7] while with the high-pressure engine no such effect can ensue.

But it is difficult to understand how any considerable quantity of hydrogen can accumulate in the boiler, since this gas, being specifically much lighter than the aqueous vapour, will naturally ascend to the top of the vessel, where the discharge-pipes are situated, and will thus be drawn with the steam to the engine before any great accumulation can take place. Moreover, it is very uncertain whether a gas

[7] Most engines have what is called a " vacuum-valve " for this very purpose.—Tr.

mixed with watery vapour would ignite at all; but be this as it may, the hydrogen gas theory is very problematical, and of late has been much more controverted than defended.

A more modern explanation of the occurrence of explosions from shortness of water in the boiler, is more probable, and more in accordance with our physical knowledge. It is founded on the supposition that the glowing metal may be suddenly covered again with water, whereby a great and instantaneous generation of steam would ensue,[8] in such quantity that none of the customary safety apparatus would avail for its timely discharge. It is easy to understand how the glowing plates may · be suddenly re-covered with water: it may happen through a sudden diminution of the pressure in the boiler; or by too great an opening of the safety-valve; or by a suddenly increased demand for steam in the engine; either of which would cause the water in the boiler to start into a state of increased ebullition,[9] and consequently to flow over the plates. This view is corroborated by the occurrence of explosions immediately after the opening of the safety-

[8] Both iron and copper generate, when red-hot, a large quantity of steam: 10 lbs. of copper, heated sufficiently to glow in the dark, convert, according to Adam Hall, 1 lb. of water into steam, which under ordinary atmospheric pressure will occupy about 27 cubic feet.

According to Marestier, 4 lbs. of red-hot iron convert 1 lb. of water into steam.

Professor Johnson, of Philadelphia, found that iron at a white heat repelled the water, and that 9 lbs. of iron, at a dull red glow, scarcely visible by daylight, converted 1 lb. of water into steam. He also remarked that cast iron generated more steam than hammered iron, in the proportion of 9 to 8¼.

[9] It has been found that by a sudden removal of the pressure in a boiler, by opening the safety-valve with the hand, the water rises in the form of a cone towards the opening, and falls suddenly back when it is closed. This would inevitably cause the re-covering of the plates with water.

valve, when the low level of the water has been remarked, and an attempt has been made to relieve the boiler from the pressure of the steam within; or when a diminished velocity of the engine has previously denoted a diminution of pressure.[10]

15. Boilers which are fitted with imperfect water gauges or feed apparatus, are particularly liable to the evils of a partial exposure of the fire surface, and unfortunately these defects are but too common, particularly with high-pressure engines. The same liability to danger is also incurred where internal fire-tubes are inserted, or where the water space is too flat and confined, and is exposed in an injudicious manner to the flues. When tubes are introduced, they seldom lie deep enough under the water level, and are therefore soon left uncovered by an accidental slight depression of the latter; and if the water chambers are too confined, the water will be often driven out during violent ebullition. Marine and locomotive boilers are particularly liable to this. A steam boat boiler which burst at Hull (an account of the accident, with a description of the appearance of the boiler after the explosion, will be found in the ' Civil Engineer and Architect's Journal,' August, 1838, p. 283) furnishes an example of such an improper make. Both imperfections were united in its construction, and the collapsed fire-tubes showed that the metal of these parts had been overheated in consequence of the water being driven out of the too contracted surrounding chambers, and that by such overheating the parts were weakened, and at last suddenly

[10] Explosions have frequently happened after the first few strokes of the engine,—a strong corroboration of the hypothesis in the text.—Tr.

gave way to the pressure. It is much to be regretted that marine boilers are usually subject to the evil of too confined and too shallow a water space; because the ship's motion renders them particularly liable to the exposure of the fire-tubes: the use of sails increases the mischief, for when the ship has lain over on one side for some time, her righting or careening will throw the water back upon any portions of the metal that may have become overheated, and thus danger may ensue in proportion to the length of time the parts have been exposed and the degree of exposure.[11]   Hence we find the majority of explosions occur on board steam boats, and proportionately but few on shore.

Now since all marine boilers, as well for low as high pressure, are liable, if injudiciously constructed, to similar dangers of the kind we have named above, no conclusion to the prejudice of high-pressure engines can be drawn from such accidents.   Indeed of late years a general comparison has been in favour of the high-pressure system.[12] One reason why low-pressure boilers must, under the evils above mentioned, be less secure than high-pressure, is

[11] The motion of the water in the large box-shaped boilers, so much in use for marine engines, entails also danger from the concussion of so great a mass set in violent motion; which often tends to damage portions of the boiler, and loosen the rivets and other joints connected with it.

[12] *Vide* 'Echo du Monde savant,' No. 24, p. 178.

Up to the year 1834, only twenty explosions had occurred in America with high-pressure engines, while thirty-two had happened with low-pressure; and it is well known how common the high-pressure engine is in that country, particularly in the Western States.

At a later date, the proprietors of steam boats in North America have stated, in a memorial to Congress, that since the more general introduction of high-pressure steam, the number of accidents has not only not increased, but become lessened in an extraordinary degree.

that in the former the ebullition is much more violent, and the water thereby more liable to be expelled, whereas under a great elasticity the bubbles of steam generated take a smaller volume, the ebullition goes on more quietly, and therefore the danger is lessened.

The common chest form of low-pressure boilers with straight sides tends to increase the liability to the exposure of parts heated by the fire, especially if furnished with internal flues, as is generally the case with marine boilers. The large flat surfaces easily bulge out by an increased pressure within, and the consequent augmentation of cubical content causes a sinking of the water surface; after which the restoration of the elasticity to its original degree may throw back the water over the spots it formerly left, and thus the source of danger is at hand.

16. It will be in place here to refer to and examine some other hypotheses brought forward to account for the explosion of steam boilers: these will moreover serve to establish the point I have in view, viz., that the high-pressure system is not less safe than the low-pressure.

To these hypotheses belong, first, that of Jacob Perkins. It has been long known that steam may be charged with an excess of free caloric,[13] when the space in which it is contained is heated from without. This may often happen when the water surface in a boiler is too low, and the metal becomes consequently incandescent in certain places. The water present does not impede this effect, because, being a bad conductor, the heat is transmitted by it very

[13] Instances are on record where, by this means, fir has been inflamed when laid on the top of a boiler, and lead joints in the engine melted. I have often found tin soldered joints in the steam-pipe melted by overheated steam.

slowly downwards. Mr. Perkins finds that such over-heated steam gains but very little in elasticity; but when water is scattered among it, and thereby becomes intimately commingled with it, (which may happen by an unusual ebullition,) the free caloric of the steam may be suddenly imparted to the water, and so may generate instantaneously steam of great elasticity in such quantity as cannot be carried off by the ordinary means of escape; and this may cause an explosion of the boiler.

This hypothesis is approved by many writers, but, for my own part, I cannot clearly see its force: for—

(1.) Should not the overheated steam escape into the engine as fast as it is created? and would it not produce such destructive effects upon the working parts as would cause immediate attention?

(2.) I do not understand how, with regular firing, the water could become so scattered among the steam as to produce the effect described. A sudden diminution of the pressure to a sufficient extent to cause a violent increase of ebullition, would be perceived by the action of the engine. The feed-pipe is always below the water level, and therefore it could not proceed from this source. And would it be so difficult for the heat to be distributed through the surface of the water, which is in constant commotion?

(3.) Some of my experiments with a steam generator made in London seem to tell against this doctrine. I have, by stopping the injection of water, kept the enclosed steam in contact with a metallic surface at a temperature of 800° Fahr., and yet no symptoms of an explosion appeared when the water was re-introduced; indeed a long-continued injection was necessary before enough pressure could be obtained to set the engine to work again. If overheated steam attains so little consequent increase of pressure, how is it that when the water falls too low in the boiler the velocity of the engine generally accelerates? I have often remarked this to be the case.

(4.) It is scarcely probable that the small quantity of steam contained in a boiler can distribute so much heat as is supposed, since it is only the *free* caloric which comes in question. Mr. Thomas Earle ('Repertory of Patent Inventions,' Suppl. Jan. 1832, page 424) calculates that this could not be enough to generate steam in any dangerous quantity.[14]

17. A second hypothesis is that of Mr. Philip Taylor (Phil. Mag. N. S. No. ii., p. 126). This appears to refer more to a forcible ejection of the boiler from its seating than to the actual explosion of the boiler itself. When by the closing of the chimney damper a quantity of coal gas is suffered to accumulate in the furnace, it may happen that by the opening of the fire door, or by other means, such a portion of atmospheric air may be admitted as will form an explosive compound by mixing with the gas; and if the fire openings are not large enough to allow of the sudden discharge, the boiler will probably be thrown from its seat. The occurrence of such explosions in badly constructed furnaces is by no means uncommon, but it is so easy a matter to provide against them by proceeding on proper principles, that they need not be further enlarged upon here.

[14] The particulars of this and other calculations to the same purpose are given by the Author in a note.—TR.

18. Thirdly, Signor Morosi maintains the extraordinary theory, that the explosion of boilers proceeds not so much from the pressure of the steam within, as from a retrocession of the steam at the moment when the piston is at its point of rest at the top or bottom of the cylinder. The whole force of the steam, he asserts, is stopped in its motion, strikes back forcibly into the boiler, like the water in the hydraulic ram, and impinges as would a solid body on the boiler plates. According to his calculations, the impinging force is equal to that of a column of water which has the surface of the boiler for its base, and pressure and velocity equal to those of the steam. The effect of this in producing explosion he likens to well-known accidents occurring with pipes to convey fluids, and he proposes many ways of avoiding the evil; but I think my own opinion of the theory, and probably that of most practical men, will justify me in omitting them here.

19. Fourthly, The electric phenomena exhibited in the discharge of high-pressure steam have lately been called to the assistance of the discussion of the question of explosions. It is suggested for consideration whether such may not take place through a great generation and sudden discharge of electric fluid, or, so to speak, by an electric shock. MM. Jobard and Tassin support this theory,[15] and adduce in its favour the explosion of a boiler at *Vieux Valesse*, which exhibited no signs of the causes of explosion generally assigned. It appears to me, however, that the hypothesis hitherto rests upon too uncertain grounds to be admitted; and I conceive we ought to post-

[15] 'Echo du Monde savant,' 1841. No. 601.

pone allowing it a place among the causes of evil until it is more certainly proved, lest we should only increase the unfounded apprehension of danger, and thus bring undeserved discredit on a good cause.

20. It must be conceded that formerly high-pressure engines were subject to more accidents, in proportion to their number, than low-pressure; but this consideration is overborne by the fact that of later years a beneficial change has taken place in favour of the high-pressure system. I have already given my opinion that the cause of the danger was always to be found in the injudicious construction of the vessels, and not in the system itself. The idea of *high-pressure* steam is only a relative one, and only has reference to the comparative strength of the vessel against which the pressure is exerted. For example, the force of high-pressure steam against a vessel of small dimensions, is not greater than that of low-pressure steam against a proportionately larger vessel. In every boiler, steam of too high an elasticity for its proportionate strength may be generated when the precautions against such an accident are neglected; but it is possible to make vessels for steam of the highest pressure of such construction that they can suffer but little from it, and therefore have the advantage over the cumbersome boilers used for low pressure. The argument that high-pressure boilers will burst sooner than low-pressure, loses all its force except on the supposition that both are of equal size and equal thickness of metal. Hereafter, when describing my own boilers, I shall enter more fully upon this consideration: suffice it now to say that both kinds of boilers may be put on a perfect equality, under ordinary

circumstances, as regards their safety; but that danger first arises when the steam considerably exceeds its proper elasticity; and that in this regard a high-pressure boiler may be constructed with a greater probability of safety than one of the other kind, if proper consideration and knowledge be brought to bear in the design. It cannot be doubted that an overstrained low-pressure boiler becomes, so to speak, a high-pressure one, and must, *cæteris paribus*, be ranked with the latter in all considerations of the consequences of accident; since what is wanting in pressure is fully compensated by its great size and the great mass of its contents. Experience has never shown that the damage arising from high-pressure explosions has exceeded that from low-pressure, and late instances have rather tended to throw the weight of evidence on the other side.

I will now endeavour to point out what are the principal and fundamental errors in the construction of high-pressure boilers, which have led in so many instances to their destruction: these I consider to be the following :—

21. First. Many high-pressure boilers are constructed of *cast iron*.[16] This is a rotten and brittle material, which, when large and thick vessels are cast from it without the greatest precautions in the operation, is very apt to become blistered and hollow, and to leave, on cooling, large air spaces invisible from the outside, but exceedingly destructive to the strength of the casting. Moreover it is

---

[16] I have seen many such in England, especially in old engines: they consist of great cylinders of 3 or 4 feet in diameter, and 6 to 10 feet long, with internal fire-tubes.

very difficult to cast large vessels of perfectly even thickness in all parts; and if they are not so, they are liable to damage when exposed to heat, from the unequal expansion and contraction of the metal, and the irregularity of changes of temperature in the different parts. It is obvious also, that when such vessels do explode, the consequences must be frightful: they resemble bombs, and the massive fragments detached seldom fail to carry destruction wherever they fly. On the contrary, forged hammered or rolled iron, as generally used for boilers, in the shape of thick plates, is strong and tenacious, and by a proper calculation of its strength may be made to offer a great resistance to the steam: it is not so liable to sudden fracture as cast iron, but usually at first gives way locally, and shows defects that bring to notice the imperfect state of the boiler, and enable timely repair to be applied.

Copper is more tough and less liable to crack than iron, and is a most excellent material for high-pressure boilers: it has, however, a less cohesive power,[17] and therefore a greater thickness of metal is necessary to produce an equal strength; but since copper boilers never fly in pieces in case of explosion, it is not necessary to be too scrupulous in regard to this point. Even when the metal is thin, especially if the diameter is not great, the use of copper removes all danger of destructive explosion, since at most only a simple tearing asunder of the metal will ensue. But more of this subject farther on.

It was formerly thought that boilers of hammered iron plate possessed the advantage above ascribed to copper;

[17] According to Guyton Morveau, in the ratio of 302 to 549.

shown that they are not entirely

» burst into pieces. Of course the

n which the danger exists depends

on the quality of the iron, and the

force.

form of boilers is not always the best.

y reasons to be cylindrical, and, when

rical ends. This form withstands best the internal pressure, because the strain is equal on all points of the circumference. It is well known how often this rule is neglected in the manufacture of high-pressure boilers. Trevithick's original large cast iron boilers were indeed cylindrical, but the ends were flat, and without any secure fastenings. The same may be said of Oliver Evans's boilers, which had moreover the defect of internal fire-tubes, a fault also possessed by the boilers of the great Cornish pumping engines. Of late the plan of flat chambers, consisting of plates tied together at many points by strong bolts, has been tried; and Mr. Walter Hancock has taken a patent for such as applied to locomotive carriages, which he finds advantageous. Occasionally we see fire-tubes of a prismoidal form introduced into high-pressure boilers,—a plan fraught with the greatest danger. I have already spoken of the disadvantages attending the use of internal fire-tubes in general.

23. Thirdly, The boilers are of too large a size. The greater the content of a boiler, the greater surface it must offer to the pressure of the steam, and the greater danger it must be subject to. This truth is so self-evident, that it is incomprehensible how it should be so universally

neglected.   The size of many boilers at present in use is truly astounding.   I have not unfrequently seen them as large as 5 or 6 feet in diameter.   Such boilers ought indeed to be named *exploders*, and the legislative restriction [18] as to the amount of pressure to be used with them is, as far as it goes, a salutary measure.   Still better would the law stand if it began at the other end, and limited the size of the vessels instead of the elasticity of the steam within them; for such an enactment would be free from the objection of discouraging the use of high-pressure steam, now promising so much advantage to industry.   We can scarcely hope, however, for the full realization of our wishes in this respect, unless a bold and enlarged view is taken of the system; for, as I shall hereafter show, the high-pressure engine cannot be made to display its advantages with steam under about six atmospheres' pressure.   A compulsory enactment restricting the size of the generating vessels would tend much towards promoting the use of steam of such high pressures, and, by producing a necessity for acquaintance with the working of the engine, would undoubtedly further its real improvement.

It is indeed customary to give to boilers of great size a proportionate thickness of metal, but this helps the case very little; for experience has shown that thick plates, especially if of cast metal, are more liable to crack by the action of the fire than thin ones; inasmuch as the temperature of their two sides, exposed respectively to the fire without and the water within, does not quickly assimilate; whereby unequal expansion and contraction ensues.   It is moreover a difficult matter to determine

[18] Probably a German one.   I know of no such law in England.—Tr.

what the proper strength ought to be in proportion to the diameter and the pressure, and there is great difference of opinion among those who have given their attention to this point. It must also be noticed, that thick vessels tend more to retard the transmission of heat to the water than thin ones, although this fact seems often to have escaped the notice of engineers.

24. Fourthly, on account of the great size of the high-pressure boilers generally made, the steam and water space in them is mostly too large and too little separated, and does not bear any consistent proportion to the dimensions of the cylinder. The great quantities of steam and water tend to produce frightful consequences in case of explosion; the former by its great pressure and sudden expansion; the latter by its instantaneous conversion into steam by the removal of the pressure; as all the free caloric beyond the boiling point is spontaneously applied to the formation of new vapour.[19]

25. Fifthly, boilers are not generally provided to a sufficient extent with safety apparatus; and such as are employed are too often improperly constructed, and kept in bad order. I have seen many examples of their defects. It is scarcely to be believed, that many of the original Trevithick boilers were not provided with safety-valves at all! The regulations which have been promulgated in many countries, with reference to the examination of safety-valves and their preservation under cover, have a useful tendency, but, as I shall hereafter show, they often

[19] This is further enlarged upon and explained by the Author.—TR.

C

fail in their object; since many accidental derangements may happen without the knowledge and in spite of the care of the attendants, and indeed may frequently occur immediately after the examination, and thus all watchfulness may be thrown away. The ordinary gauges for the pressure or temperature of the steam are only useful if constantly observed, and yet how seldom are they noticed by the majority of engine attendants. Certain contrivances have been invented which should ring a bell, or open a valve, or perform some such precautionary measure when the elasticity has risen to a certain height; but these only add complexity to a system which ought to be in the highest degree simple; and moreover, many of such contrivances are only applicable to low-pressure steam.

Metallic plugs, fusible at a low temperature, have been revived of late years, and their use is prescribed and regulated in France by law. But these are open to many objections: they often become dangerously softened before they reach the temperature at which they are destined to give way; and they only serve at best but as indices for the *temperature* of the steam, and as preventives against its overheating. Thus in case of a partial overheating of the metal of the boiler, and consequent surcharge of the steam with caloric, one of these plugs would become rather a disadvantage than otherwise, as it would, by its melting and allowing the steam to rush out, cause such a violent ebullition by the diminution of the pressure, as would probably bring about the very explosion it was the object of the precaution to prevent.

26. *Second Objection against the High-pressure Engine.* This is, that in the use of high-pressure steam much heat

is wasted, and therefore a greater expenditure of fuel is required than for low-pressure.

Although the fallacy of this opinion has been most fully shown in America, and later in France, by the most convincing and incontrovertible facts, the objection is still laid great stress on, especially in England, where the use of locomotive engines has, by their great consumption of fuel, rather increased than lessened the prejudice against the principle. The little that is said in its favour has but a remote chance of being attended to among such objections, and even the late extraordinary performances of the Cornish engines have either been disbelieved, or, where received in a better spirit, have produced but a trifling interest in favour of the use of high-pressure steam.

I will now give the statements which have formed the grounds of the objection alluded to, and investigate whether these are or are not of sufficient weight to render the allegation of serious import; and in so doing I shall principally call experience to my aid.

27. First. It is said that in heating any high-pressure steam generator, much heat must necessarily escape unused out of the furnace, since no heated currents which are below the temperature of the generator itself and its contents can give off heat to them.

Now I have found by experience that the evaporation of fluids will often draw off so much heat from bodies with which they are in contact, that these bodies may attain a very low temperature. Examples of this may be found in the cold experienced by the hand when volatile fluids are placed upon it;—by the conversion of water into ice by the evaporation of ether in vacuo;—by the cooling of water in earthen vessels through moistening the outside;—and lastly, by the experiment of placing the hand at the bottom of a vessel of boiling water just removed from the fire, when almost the whole of the heat will appear to be drawn off by the ebullition.

These results seem to suggest the question whether the evaporating fluid may not bring the surrounding bodies, from which it draws its supply of caloric, down to a lower temperature than itself, and thus allow more heat to be withdrawn from the gases in the furnace than the objection supposes.

But it has also been found by experience that steam has been raised at a pressure of two atmospheres in one of Perkins's boilers, while the hand might be held in the smoke current passing off into the chimney; and I have myself seen the same thing. I have frequently placed my hand in the exit-flue of my boilers, and held it there some time without feeling more than a supportable and not disagreeable warmth; yet, however, it is a singular circumstance, and one which at present I cannot satisfactorily explain, that the thermometer showed, when placed in this current, a temperature equal to that of the steam in the boiler.[20] It has been asserted that a current heated as high as 400° Fahr. is necessary in order to produce a sufficient draught in the chimney, but my experience has shown me that a much less temperature will answer the purpose; and if this assertion were true it would evidently get rid of the objection we are considering, since low-pressure engines must then be subject to a

[20] It is well known to those who have had to do with the warming and ventilating of buildings, that a current of air of high temperature produces a very deceptive effect upon any part of the human body exposed to it.—Tr.

greater waste than high-pressure, in order to secure the draught in the furnace. It cannot be denied that in too many instances this loss does take place with both kinds of engines; but I shall hereafter find occasion to show how this arises, and to prove that it is unnecessary under a proper system of management and construction.[21]

M. Christian, of Paris, to whom we owe many of the latest researches in the theory of steam, found that equal quantities of water were evaporated in equal times, by the same fire, under various pressures and temperatures.[22] Now since the mechanical effect of a given quantity of water as steam when used to produce power varies in value according to the pressure, and always gives the advantage to steam of *high* pressure, so is it clear that in proportion to the power obtained there is not only no loss, but rather a gain in the economy of fuel.[23]   I have often

[21] The best answer to this objection has been overlooked by the Author. It is found in the fact that such arrangements of the boiler and heating surface may and ought to be made, that the portions of the current impinging *last* upon the boiler before escaping into the chimney, may act upon the *coolest* portions of the water, namely, such as are newly introduced by the feed. This is admirably managed in the Cornish boilers: as see 'Treatise on the Cornish Engine' by the Translator, Arts. 129 to 131.—Tr.

[22] And so did Watt long before him.   The Author gives in a long note the opinions of various writers on the disputed point of the quantity of heat in steam; but as the discussion is well known in England, I have not transcribed his remarks.   He vouches from his own experiments to the correctness of that view of the case which is, I believe, most generally received in England;—that the *sum* of the sensible and latent heats is *constant* at all pressures, and equal to 650° centigrade.—Tr.

[23] I have investigated this point in the beginning of the third part of my work on the Cornish Engine, where my object is to show that the use of high-pressure steam, *per se*, is one of the causes of the great economy of that engine. This is demonstrated very clearly by a simple form of algebraical expression for the relation between the density and the pressure of the steam, and also by a practical arithmetical example.—Tr.

remarked that my engines worked with the least consumption of fuel when I had the throttle-valve least open,
and consequently raised the pressure in the boiler higher
than usual; and although the expansive working of the
steam in the cylinder might be advantageous, this was not
sufficient to explain the whole gain : we may at least draw
the conclusion that an increase of pressure did not produce any disadvantage in such a case.   It will generally
be found that an engine works more economically when
fully loaded than when working under power, and this
is again in favour of the more economical generation of
steam of high elasticity.

But certain experiments which I have made with a
generator obtained in England for steam of very great
elasticity, have shown in the most positive and unequivocal manner the fallacy of the objection; for I have been
able to convert, with one pound of coal, 8 to 10 ℔s. of
ice-cold water into steam of from 600 ℔s. to 800 ℔s.
pressure per square inch.   During the evaporation there
was so little heat passing away, that even after a long use
of the apparatus I have scarcely found the 9-inch walls of
the chimney warm : and I have now engines at work that
lose very little; I have indeed found that the waste heat
applied to the feed water in a vessel of extended surface,
would not raise it up to 40° Reaumur.

With respect to the use of a blast in the furnace of high-
pressure generators, I am inclined to think it an advantage, inasmuch as it tends to produce a more perfect combustion than when the fire is allowed to burn slowly.   Too
little attention is paid to secure this end in ordinary cases,
and frequently a great deal of trouble is taken to remove
an evil that has its source in a different cause from those

to which the remedies are applied. The most important principle upon which improvement in the furnace can be based has been shown by Herr Wagenmann. The smoke can only be completely burned by causing the perfect mixture of the gases over the furnace before an abstraction of heat takes place by contact with the comparatively cold surfaces of the boiler. If the current is allowed to cool, and to be mixed with a quantity of cold atmospheric air, admitted through other openings than the interstices of the fire, it is next to impossible that perfect combustion can take place. It is especially disadvantageous in this respect to have the furnace placed inside the boiler, a practice which, on account of its convenience, and its requiring no masonry, is usually adopted on board steam vessels. It is supposed to be an economical plan, because the heat which is in other cases expended on the brickwork, in this arrangement goes to heat the boiler; but the idea of its economy is a mistaken one, for the cooling of the fire currents against the sides of the boiler before perfect combustion has taken place causes more loss than the absence of the brick-work causes gain. The frightful clouds of smoke which pour from most of our steamers justify the explanation we have given of their almost universal want of economy.

M. Balcourt has put on record a very remarkable observation, made on a steam engine erected at New Orleans. He found that it would only do half its work when the fire-grate was raised six inches above its customary level. This is quite explicable on the hypothesis, that in the higher position the gases came in contact with the then nearer surface of the boiler before they were perfectly consumed; whereby they lost the heat necessary for their incandescence, and imperfect combustion was the consequence.

It has been lately attempted to prevent loss of heat from the furnace of a boiler, either by passing the feed water through vessels exposed to the exit current, or by dividing the boiler into several parts which are acted upon by the heat in turn, the feed water being introduced into the last of the course. Both these plans have the advantage that the smoke current acts last upon the coolest water, and thereby affords the best chance of all the available heat being withdrawn.[24]   Another important circumstance in favour of such arrangements is that the feed-pump may work with cold water, which obviates many evils constantly liable to arise when this important apparatus is made to work in hot water.

28. Secondly. Another argument made use of to support the objection that the high-pressure engine is not economical in fuel is derived from the great loss of radiant heat which these engines are said to suffer. Inasmuch as this loss from the surface of a heated body is greater as the surface is hotter; and inasmuch as many of the high-pressure boilers commonly constructed expose more surface to the outer atmosphere than they do to the fire, the argument must be admitted to have some force, especially as we so often see locomotive engines exposed carelessly to the weather. But it is easily shown that proper care in the construction and arrangements will remove the objection; and as I shall have ample occasion to enlarge

[24] Here we are again irresistibly reminded of the Cornish arrangements.— Tr.

upon this in a future part of the work, I shall say no more of it in this place.

29. Thirdly, another cause of waste of heat is said to be, that in consequence of the great pressure, there is more leakage of steam at the piston and joints of the engine, than with low pressure. This objection also depends, as to its value, entirely upon the state of the machine, and has no weight if the engine is well constructed and kept in good repair. It cannot, however, be said, unfortunately, that later engines have improved in this respect; and this, I think, is to be ascribed principally to the descriptions of pistons that have been introduced in late days, and that have often proved the reverse of improvements. Experiments of this kind are always useful in the search after truth; but we may profit by the experience already gained with the condensing engine, and we can never be at a loss for a perfectly tight piston if we adhere to the old hemp packing, and adapt it in a suitable manner to the wants of the high-pressure engine. As to the other joints, they present no difficulty but what may easily be surmounted by using the proper materials in a proper manner. And fortunately in the high-pressure engine we have to do with joints of much smaller dimensions, and therefore of much easier management than with low-pressure. My recommendation of the return to hemp pistons may, perhaps, at first sight appear a retrograde step, but I think it will be justified by what I shall hereafter advance, and that experience will corroborate all I assert in its favour. In the search after truth we often find ourselves compelled to relinquish what we have erroneously considered as better because

it is novel, and to return to older and more long-tried plans.

30. *Third Objection against the High-pressure Engine.* This is, that it does not realize the advantages of the vacuum obtained in condensing engines. If it could be shown that this vacuum was formed and maintained in low-pressure engines without sacrifice of power, the objection would have more weight; but experience tells us that partly through imperfect condensation, partly through the working of the air and cold water pumps, and from other causes of the same description, the useful effect of low-pressure engines is reduced from about 17 ℔s. per square inch absolute pressure upon the piston, to about *seven*, as made available in power obtained;[25] so that the use of condensation only in reality offers a gain of from 4½ to 5 ℔s. per square inch, or one-third of the atmospheric pressure. It must then be admitted, that such a comparatively small gain is more than compensated by the advantages peculiar to the high-pressure engine; such, for example, as the greatly diminished prejudicial resistance; the simpler construction and smaller size in proportion to the power; the absence of so many pumps, pump-rods, and other machinery; the smaller mass to be set and kept in motion; the smaller proportionate diameter of the cylinder; the consequent diminution of friction of the piston, &c., &c.

The objection loses in weight as we use steam of higher pressure, and at seven or eight atmospheres is scarcely to

[25] Modern engines have much more *real* power than this: 7 ℔s. per square inch is used for the *nominal* power, which is generally much under what is actually performed. The argument, however, is good as far as it goes.—Tr.

ѕe considered, because the surface of the piston becomes
ᵽroportionately less as the elasticity is increased, and there-
ᶠore the loss of the vacuum is less to be felt; while the
ᶐdvantages of the system are increased by such increase of
ᶒlasticity. When the pressure used is too low, for example,
ᶆnly two or three atmospheres, as is most common, the
ᶩoss may be important, and the advantages of the high-
ᵽressure system are not sufficiently developed to cover it.
ᶠor instance, an engine of 10-horse power at two atmo-
pheres' pressure, will require about twice as much steam as
ₐ condensing one of the same power: it must be of about
ₕhe same dimensions, and by the want of a vacuum must
ᵦe supplied with steam of a double elasticity to produce the
ₛame effect. Here, therefore, a power of ten horses will
ᵦe sacrificed by the want of the vacuum; that is, as much
ₐs the whole power of the engine. But if a pressure of
ᵢight or ten atmospheres be used, and the principle of ex-
ᵽansion applied, the proportionate loss, by the sacrifice of
ₜhe vacuum, will be scarcely equal to 2-horse power out of
ten,—a loss of very trifling weight when compared with the
advantages possessed by such an engine over a low-pressure one. Yet more in favour of the high-pressure engine
would the comparison be if we could substitute steam of
sixteen atmospheres for that of eight; but unfortunately,
through practical difficulties in the working of the machinery, our limits of available elasticity are at present too
confined.

31. *Fourth Objection against the High-pressure Engine.*
This is, that a greater consumption of oil and grease is
required for lubrication of the piston, piston-rod, and valve
apparatus, than for engines of low pressure. This objec-

tion is sometimes enhanced by the assertion, that the grease becomes volatilized at the temperature of steam of very high pressure.

Now since fat, animal as well as vegetable, only boils at a temperature of 220° Reaumur (527° Fahrenheit), and moreover does not, like water, volatilize at a heat under that of ebullition, it can scarcely be conceived how any loss can take place by volatilization in engines working up to eight or ten atmospheres, where only about half the above-named heat exists; and this pressure I never recommend to be exceeded. Experience has never shown the justice of the assertion, if we except a case mentioned by Mr. Perkins, where the grease (equal parts of good olive oil and Russia tallow) used for the piston was said to become partially decomposed; but this was under a much higher pressure than eight or ten atmospheres; and I must say in opposition, that I have never observed such a result when working up to forty atmospheres; but rather that an unusually small portion of grease, not the eighth part of what is necessary for low-pressure engines, was required.

I account for the loss of grease, when it exists, by waste merely, and not by evaporation or decomposition. The oleaginous particles become intimately mixed with the particles of water that lodge upon the sides of the cylinder, and are then blown away with the steam in its exit from the engine. This is the reason why the water which collects in the escape-pipes presents a milky or soapy appearance. It is a mistake to imagine that the black indurating substance that impure grease often leaves in the cylinder, and which is often so injurious both to the packing and the metal, arises from the decomposition of the fatty matter; for this substance is nothing more than an induration of the fleshy particles left in impure tallow. It has been attempted to purify the tallow by the use of sulphuric acid in the melting, but this process frequently leaves free acid among the grease, which is very destructive to the parts of the engine.

According to my experience, a high-pressure engine requires much *less* lubrication for the packings of the piston and piston-rod than a low-pressure one. If it is once shown that the grease neither evaporates nor decomposes under the temperature, it is easily proved that the consumption *must* be less, inasmuch as the rubbing surfaces are so much smaller, according to the power. If the proprietors of high-pressure engines complain of the consumption, it must be because the attendants waste the material. The milky appearance of the water in the exit-pipes is common with low-pressure as well as with high-pressure engines, and, as already remarked, furnishes a conclusion against the decomposition theory.

32. *Fifth Objection.*—This is, that the working parts of high-pressure engines are more subject to wear and tear, and, as a consequence, that the engines themselves are more liable to interruptions in their working from the necessity of repairs.

This objection I can only allow to apply to those parts which are subject during their friction to an excessive degree of heat. But my experience has shown me, that with a pressure not exceeding eight to ten atmospheres the friction of such surfaces causes no disadvantage unless accompanied by too great an increase of pressure upon them; in such cases, for example, as the slide-valves when injudiciously constructed, and the axes of oscillating cylinders when the steam is made to pass through them to and from the cylinder. I have in my earlier writings shown how these rubbing heated surfaces might be got rid of,[26] but the method is not without difficulty; and a longer practice in the manufacture of engines has convinced me that my former opinions required a change, and that the use of slide-valves was more convenient and more to be depended upon in many points of view than that of seat-valves. The latter are apt to be caused to leak by impurities in the grease,—by small portions of hemp from the packings of the pistons or stuffing-boxes,—or by other strange intruding bodies; and when this happens, great loss is occasioned, owing to the penetrating property of high-pressure steam, and the facility with which it will make its escape through the smallest openings. I do not deny that formerly I had much antipathy to slide-valves, principally because I at that time advocated the use of steam of a very high elasticity; but since I have been compelled, as an actual engine manufacturer, to adopt a cautious and secure line of practice, in order to be able to give the necessary guarantees for my work, I have devoted more attention generally to established and long-tried apparatus, and among them to the slide-valve; and in order to induce more certainty in the action of this essential organ, I have reduced and regulated the pressure under which my engines ordinarily work. I have been well satisfied with the results of my proceeding in this matter; for while I have realized in an ample measure the advantages of the high-pressure engine, I have avoided the inconveniences and

---

[26] Principally by the substitution of *seat-valves* for the *slide*.—Tr.

difficulties which in certain cases attach to the use of steam of very great elasticity.

It is inconceivable how the apparatus for transmitting the motion of the piston of a high-pressure engine to the machinery can be more subject to destruction, in regard to the durability of its joints, than in a low-pressure. If the power of each be the same, the machinery must have in each case equal strength: the stress to which it is subject is the same (or rather is less in the high-pressure engine, on account of the diminished prejudicial resistance, and consequently diminished total pressure required), and there is no reason whatever why any required strength may not be given to these parts; so that if there should be apprehension from the unequal action of the piston when expansion is used, the strength may be increased at pleasure. Can the gradually diminishing force of the steam of an expanding engine do more mischief than the great shock which must occur in low-pressure engines, owing to their increased resistance? Then every one knows what sudden concussions are produced throughout the machinery of a condensing engine at the moment when the air-pump discharges its contents, at which instant the whole pressure of the atmosphere is suddenly thrown upon the area of the pump. This shock is generally so forcible as to cause the whole machine to tremble, and to make itself heard for a long distance. Such a shock must undeniably tend to produce more damage to the moving parts than any cause which can be inherent in the high-pressure engine, whose simplicity and compactness are such as to give every facility for the attainment of the greatest security in its action, and the utmost durability in its mechanical arrangements.

It must, however, be confessed, that the construction of the high-pressure engine as usually adopted in England, has tended to bring discredit on the principle in regard to the durability of the machines. It has been frequently the practice, in order to gain an agreeable appearance and form, to fall into the great error of adopting the same proportions of the parts to each other as are used for the low-pressure engine : if these are regulated, as has often been done, by the diameter of the cylinder, according to the low-pressure calculations, the whole must of necessity be too weak, and subject to untimely destruction. The English have been much too negligent in their treatment of high-pressure engines, and thence it is that we cannot take their examples for our guidance with this machine, as we are wont to do with their low-pressure engines.[27]

ADVANTAGES OF THE HIGH-PRESSURE ENGINE.

33. Having now answered some of the most weighty objections brought against the high-pressure engine, and having shown in the course of the investigation that this

---

[27] This allegation is but too commonly true, or at least is not without good foundation. Such mistakes may be traced in the majority of cases to the (miscalled) *practical* method of working, so often approved and recommended by ignorant men. It has been too much the fashion to decry the study of *principles*, and to trust to what is called the " rule of thumb " line of practice, derived from experience *only*. This may answer very well of course while the party trusting to it confines his efforts to imitating what has been already done ; but when any thing new has to be provided for, unless the Engineer has a knowledge of *principles* to guide him, and a capability too of reasoning upon those principles, he has no alternative but to blunder on till he arrives by hazard at the desired result. This would matter but little to any except the party himself, if his trials were private ; but unhappily in most cases the unfortunate public have to pay for the schooling of their Engineer, and to suffer from the blunders his ignorance has caused.—Tr.

machine requires considerable modification from the existing methods of construction, in order to free it from its present defects; and having, moreover, referred to the possibility of effecting such beneficial changes;—I will now proceed to enumerate the peculiar advantages derivable from the use of this simple and valuable method of employing steam power; hoping thereby to turn the attention of future improvers as much as possible towards the laudable object of its yet more extended application. If what I have already said may contribute to turn these efforts in a right course, and to point out the most important principles from which improvement must proceed, I shall be amply repaid for the work I have undertaken; and I am the more induced to hope this may be the result, since it is upon the foundation here laid I have based the improvements which I myself have effected in the machine.

34. To the great advantages which high-pressure engines present over those of low pressure belong the following.

First Advantage.—They are much more simple, and, in proportion to their power, are of much smaller size, and much less weight. They are therefore less costly in the first instance, and less expensive to maintain in action; they are more compact, and occupy less room. For the cylinder is much smaller in diameter for an equal power; the length of the stroke may be also generally less; and, since condensation is not required, the velocity of the piston may usually be greater, by which means many parts of the machinery, particularly the fly-wheel, may be diminished in weight and dimensions. It is obvious also, that much of the heavy apparatus of the condensing engine is altogether absent in the high-pressure one; such, for example, as the condenser with its appurtenances; the air-pump, the hot and cold water pumps, and all the complicated appendages necessary to attach these to the main beam of the engine. Moreover, all the troublesome and expensive arrangements for condensing water are dispensed with, such as cisterns, excavations, channels, and pipes, to convey the cold water to, and the waste water from, the machine. Many pistons and valves requiring constant watchfulness to keep them tight, are unnecessary in the high-pressure engine; and thus not only the trouble but the materials for packing and lubrication are saved. In the jointing of pipes much also is spared. The various parts are much less clumsy and awkward to manage, and therefore the engines are more portable, and their erection becomes much more convenient and easy. This latter qualification has caused their exclusive use for locomotives and steam carriages.

It must, however, be remarked, that all the above-enumerated advantages apply to the *engines* alone, and do not always refer in the same degree to the *boilers*. The dimensions of these do not follow the smaller size of the cylinder in the same proportion; but still, as a smaller actual quantity of water is required to be evaporated, they have their advantages when properly constructed. In the unscientific arrangements heretofore generally adopted for the generation of high-pressure steam, the boilers have been most formidable objects of attention, requiring enormous strength and weight of metal, and the greatest trouble in manufacture; but these inconveniences may be much reduced, as I shall hereafter show, by a more suitable method of construction.

35. *Second Advantage.*—The high-pressure engine sustains much less loss from the friction and other prejudicial resistances inherent in the engine itself, than is the case with the condensing engine. The rubbing surfaces are neither so numerous nor so large; there are not so many bearings and journals; several pistons are absent, and those that do exist are smaller. The fly-wheel is of less weight, and therefore the friction of its bearings is less. The air and cold water pumps, which consume so much power in the condensing engine, are wanting. The only pistons in the high-pressure engine are the steam piston and the feed-pump, and the friction of these is very insignificant in proportion to the work done.[28]

36. *Third Advantage.*—High-pressure engines do not require the constant large supply of cold water necessary for condensation. This, in many situations and under circumstances which often occur, is very difficult to be obtained; and even where it can be had, often requires extensive excavations, pipes and conduits, and frequently also apparatus for cooling the water discharged from the engine. All these arrangements increase to a very considerable extent the first outlay. Steam vessels also, which visit tropical climates, often find it difficult to obtain water sufficiently cold for efficient condensation. The advantages of the high-pressure engine in this respect have never hitherto been sufficiently estimated.

37. *Fourth Advantage.*—Although high-pressure engines

---

[28] Some paragraphs, which, in the original, follow here, I have incorporated with the *eighth* advantage.—Tr.

demand, when a considerable elasticity is used, a greater degree of care and accuracy in the fitting of the joints, in order to make them steam-tight, they yet possess this great advantage, that leakage is sooner discovered in them than in low-pressure engines. In the former a failure, or aperture, however small, is at once betrayed, and can be immediately attended to; but with the latter, leakages, especially of air into the vacuous space, may continue for a great length of time without discovery.

38. *Fifth Advantage.*—In the high-pressure engine, the operation of *blowing through* at starting, by which both time and steam are lost, is not required. The pressure of air in the engine, at the commencement of its motion, is rather an advantage than otherwise, as when expanded by the heat, it serves to assist the motion.

39. *Sixth Advantage.*—The use of high-pressure steam allows, at any time when desired, a temporary augmentation of the usual power of the engine, without any other preparation or alteration than that of a slightly increased production of steam in the boiler. All the parts are constantly in readiness to receive, and to apply, a higher pressure of steam. It is, however, not so with the condensing engine. The condensation is only adapted for a certain quantity of steam each stroke, and if a larger amount were to be thrown in, the consequence would be an imperfect exhaustion of the cylinder, which would neutralize any attempt to increase the power of the engine by an augmented pressure of the steam. It is on this account that the high-pressure engine is invaluable for locomotive purposes. The advantages we are now in-

sisting on may be best attained by making the boiler of
such dimensions and strength as will suffice for an increased pressure of steam; and when this preparation is
made, the ordinary working of the engine will be managed
by a careful adjustment of the firing to a degree between
maximum and minimum.   Mr. Gurney proposed to use
in the boilers of his locomotive carriages, steam of a high
pressure, which was *wire-drawn* to two or three atmospheres in the engine by a diminution of the opening of
the throttle-valve.   When therefore he wished to increase
the power of his engine, all he had to do was to open this
valve a little wider, by which means he proposed to adapt
his engine to overcome the ascent of hills.   This plan of
wire-drawing the steam is doubtless a favourable one in
regard to economy.

40. *Seventh Advantage.*—High-pressure engines have
also the great advantage, that the state of the packing of
the piston, as to whether it is steam-tight, or to what
extent leakage exists, may be easily discovered by the
manner in which the steam blows out from the cylinder.
In order to render this observation more convenient, I
make a small opening in the discharge-tube, which is
usually stopped with a wooden plug: when the stopper
is withdrawn, the steam blows through the hole in the
same manner as through the large tube itself, and can be
observed accordingly.   In low-pressure engines, it must
be allowed that the greater or less heat of the condensed
water gives an index of the same important condition,
but this is neither so direct as the method just described,
nor so much to be depended on; since the quantity or
temperature of the injection water may often change, the

former depending, in fact, constantly on the state of the vacuum.

41. *Eighth Advantage.*—The high-pressure engine is more economical in fuel. This advantage is developed partly in the generation of the high-pressure steam, partly in consequence of its more suitable application to its purpose in the machine itself.

For the positive determination of the reality of this important but much doubted fact, we are indebted principally to the Americans and the French, who have paid more attention, theoretically and practically, to the high-pressure engine, than the English, and are therefore more competent judges in such a weighty matter.

But the advantage is not only proved by experience, but is deducible also from theory. It has already been long known that the temperature and elasticity of aqueous vapour increased in a ratio favourable to the practical application of high-pressure steam; and therefore it has been conjectured, as now is shown to be the fact, that engines on this principle ought to be more economical than those of low pressure. I have already (Art. 27) alluded to the subject of the caloric in high and low-pressure steam, and I may add here, that if it is proved that the former contains most free caloric, this is an advantage, rather than the contrary, inasmuch as the greater or less elasticity of the vapour is not the effect of its density alone, but also of its expansion by the free caloric it contains. In this regard, the saving of latent heat in highly elastic steam undeniably outweighs the disadvantage of a greater necessary supply of free caloric.

The expansion of high-pressure steam by its greater

content of free caloric has been occasionally doubted; but its greater proportionate useful effect, even when separated from all other causes of advantage that can occur in the machine, speaks in favour of the hypothesis. My experience has shown me, that in considering the effect of high-pressure steam, something more than the density must be taken into account; and the fact of its exceedingly great subtilty and penetrating power, in which respect it is beyond comparison with any other highly compressed fluid, as air for example, confirms me in this opinion.

It is usually considered that steam increases in volume by the addition of free caloric, in the same ratio as atmospheric air; that is (according to Bernouilli) about $\frac{1}{270}$ ($\frac{1}{267}$) of its original volume at freezing point, for each degree centigrade. But is not this proportion too small for high-pressure steam? My experiments, as well as those of others, lead me to think so, and I am of opinion, that if steam supercharged with free caloric could be used in an engine much economy would result. At present, however, such a plan could scarcely be tried without destruction to the packings and other working parts of the machine.[29]

42. Secondly, the peculiar economy of the high-pressure engine arises also from a more suitable application of the steam to its purpose in the engine itself: and this on the following grounds.

(*a.*) The steam finds less resistance to its action in this

[29] I do not quite see that the Author makes out his case conclusively in this Article; but I refer again to my own demonstration (see note to Art. 27) that the use of high-pressure steam, *per se*, is advantageous in regard to economy.—TR.

engine; for on account of the great pressure, its motion
to and from the cylinder is more free and rapid than in
the low-pressure engine.   In the latter the condensation
proceeds gradually, and therefore at the commencement
of the stroke the resistance to the piston is much greater
than when the steam has had time to condense more
perfectly.[30]   This defect, which in my opinion is one of
the causes of the loss of useful effect in condensing
engines, has, I think, been generally too much neglected,
and I will therefore explain my meaning a little more
fully.

It is obvious that, in order to gain the full effect from
the action of the steam upon the piston, the pressure
opposed to its motion ought to be removed as quickly
and as completely as possible, and therefore at the commencement of every stroke the steam remaining from
the last one should be withdrawn with all possible
rapidity.   Now in the high-pressure engine this may
be completely accomplished by the mere precaution of
making the steam passages of sufficient size and allowing them to open quickly;[31] but in the condensing

[30] We may again refer to the peculiar advantages of the Cornish engine,
where the *pause* before the commencement of the stroke is especially adapted
to the removal of the defect mentioned in the text,—a defect very generally
existing in the ordinary Boulton and Watt engines.   The *lead* often given to
the slide-valve of rotating engines also contributes in some degree to mitigate
the evil.—Tr.

[31] I have often remarked in my steam engines (where the steam makes
its exit from the cylinder with a pressure of about three atmospheres) the
singular circumstance that at the moment of the exit of the steam, a grease-
valve on the cylinder, opening inwards, *let in air;* showing thereby that the
pressure within at that moment was less than that of the atmosphere.   I
explain this by the inertia of the steam, which, being once set in violent
motion, continues it somewhat beyond the point where the pressure becomes
equal to that of the atmosphere.   This circumstance gives a satisfactory answer

engine there are several impediments in the way, which I will enumerate briefly.

(1.) The valve motion is much too sluggish. The apparatus is generally worked by an eccentric on the fly-shaft, and the opening is only fully completed when the engine has made half its stroke.

(2.) The exhaustion openings are usually made much too small in proportion to the size of the cylinder. I shall have occasion to speak further on this point.

(3.) The communications with the condenser are also too confined, so that the steam cannot pass away with sufficient rapidity.[32]

(4.) By the ordinary method of injection the condensation is not effected instantaneously, but gradually, by reason that the quantity of water necessary to condense the cylinder-full of steam must occupy some considerable time in passing through the injection cock. Therefore there remains a counter-pressure against the piston, greatest at the commencement of the stroke, and gradually diminishing as more water is injected and the condensation becomes more perfect. It is attempted to improve this state of things by increasing the injection opening, but this entails the disadvantage of requiring a greater quantity of water to be supplied and withdrawn than is proportionate to the quantity of steam to be condensed.

---

to the objection derived from the supposed greater counter-pressure on the piston, and corroborates the asserted advantages of the high-pressure engine over the condensing one.

[32] These three defects of course may be rectified. In an engine which I altered in these respects, I doubled the velocity by this means alone. I shall hereafter give rules for the best proportions.

Thus may be explained, on the one hand, the imperfect vacuum observed in some engines; and on the other, the excess of the actual over the calculated quantity of condensing water necessary to be supplied.

From these and other causes we find about one-half of the total power of the steam absorbed in the condensing engine: *i. e.* out of 17 ℔s. total pressure, only about 7 ℔s. are made available for useful effect; while with the high-pressure engine, when properly constructed, I can vouch by my own experience, that only *one-fourth* need be so consumed. Others have sometimes found the loss greater, but I believe they have always been misled by the use of engines of an inferior description.

(*b.*) M. Christian, of Paris, has found by direct experiment,[33] that the loss of power consequent upon increasing the velocity of the piston is proportionately much less in the high-pressure engine than in the low-pressure; and that the mechanical effect in respect to the higher velocity is increased to a greater extent as the pressure used is greater. This is corroborated by the well-known fact, that the piston of a high-pressure engine may be driven at a great velocity (250 to 300 feet per minute) without entailing the loss which always ensues when the velocity of the low-pressure engine exceeds about 200 feet per minute.

(*c.*) The use of high-pressure steam allows the prin-

---

[33] *Vide* 'Traité de Mechan. industrielle,' by this Author, p. 345. His researches are very interesting, and I recommend them to attention.

ciple of expansion to be carried to a greater extent than in the low-pressure engine, without requiring the dimensions of the cylinder to be considerably increased. By the application of this principle a most important saving is attained; but that it cannot be carried out efficiently with low-pressure steam, is shown by the fact, that the sagacious WATT could not work it to advantage, and that WOOLF, who re-introduced it with success, used high-pressure steam in his engines. When the expansion principle is used with low-pressure steam, the effective pressure is so small that the cylinder must be greatly increased in size to give a certain power. To this cause may also be traced the failure of Hornblower's engines, which were expansion engines with low-pressure steam, and on which Woolf afterwards so much improved.[34]

(d.) The steam acts in a manner, so to speak, altogether *positive*, and is not robbed of all that valuable portion of heat which in the low-pressure engine is lost by condensation. On this account the steam, after passing from the engine, may be used again for a variety of purposes; such as for warming the feed water before it enters the boiler; for the purposes of cooking, heating buildings, drying, &c. In certain manufactories where large pans or boilers, drying apparatus, &c., require to be heated, the power of an engine may be obtained almost free of expense by adopting the plan above named.[35]

---

[34] For a further illustration of these remarks, see 'Treatise on the Cornish Engine,' Arts. 40 to 46.—TR.

[35] I have for the last twenty-five years directed my attention to this point, and have had the opportunity of contriving many uses, of greater or less

(*e.*) There is not so great a degree of condensation in the cylinder. According to my idea, the views generally adopted on this subject hitherto have been entirely erroneous. It is given as a principle, that steam at a high temperature is more exposed to condensation than when at a lower degree of heat, since the transmission of caloric from one body to another is quicker as the difference between their temperatures is greater; but it has been overlooked, that in low-pressure engines there exists a circumstance which appears to me to be a greater cause of waste of heat, and which I will endeavour briefly to explain.

In the low-pressure engine, the vapour in condensing gradually becomes attenuated before it finally leaves the cylinder, and by this attenuation it loses proportionately in temperature: further, the steam acquires by being thus cooled a tendency to rob the cylinder of the heat previously given to it by the steam newly admitted, and thereby to take into the condenser more free caloric than would naturally belong to its elasticity. That WATT, and subsequently WOOLF, overlooked this circumstance, is shown by their use of the steam-jacket, by which this disadvantage was naturally increased.[36] It has been often subject of astonishment why the quantity of water necessary for condensation should

---

importance, for the waste steam from the high-pressure engine: these I shall hereafter notice.

[36] We are yet much in the dark as to the precise nature and degree of the influence of the steam-jacket over the action of the steam within the cylinder of expanding engines; but it seems to be well ascertained that a casing of steam is absolutely necessary to the economical working of the Cornish engine. The experiments made upon it in Cornwall have just sufficed to establish this point, and no more.—TR.

always be found in practice greater than that given by calculation, and the error has generally been laid to the charge of leakage in the piston packing; but it seems to me that the fact is explained by the reason I have given. If then this abstraction of heat from the metal of the cylinder be allowed to exist, it is easily understood what a loss must be sustained by the newly entering steam which has to furnish the supply to compensate for such abstraction. When a steam-jacket is used, of course this loss falls upon the steam inside the jacket.

But, it may be asked, does not a loss of a similar kind also exist in the high-pressure engine? Certainly; but it must be considered that the surface of the cylinder in this engine bears a much smaller proportion to the volume of the steam discharged; and that the exit is too rapid, and renewed too quickly, to allow of any considerable abstraction of heat, which must be a work of time. Besides, this loss is less noticeable in engines where expansion is used, and where the steam is applied to other purposes after it has been discharged from the engine.

43. Having now set forth the principal advantages of the high-pressure engine, I must finally say a few words for the purpose of correcting certain mistaken ideas which are very prevalent, even among enlightened and scientific men, in reference to the source whence economy of fuel in the machine should arise.

It has been the general opinion that this source lay in the generation of the steam, and to this end have most of the later improvements been directed; while the engine itself and the principles of its construction have been thought to have but little influence in the matter.[37]   Now although I have certainly endeavoured to show that there is an undeniable advantage to be derived from the use of high-pressure steam, considered in respect to the economy of its production, and moreover that this advantage increases with the pressure employed; yet must I strongly protest against the erroneous idea, that the greatest improvement of the high-pressure engine is to be looked for in the more perfect arrangement of the apparatus for its generation. The advantages to be derived from the suitable application of the steam in the machine are to me so clear and obvious, that I have, in what I have done, had more respect to this point than to the economy of the boiler: it will, however, be found that in the details which I shall exhibit in the following pages, I have endeavoured to apply and carry out, to the utmost extent, all the principles of improvement I have hereinbefore laid down.

[37] It is worthy of remark, that nearly all modern inventions directed towards the improvement of the high-pressure engine, and particularly all those described in the latest English patents, have had reference to the boiler alone. This shows how little has been thought of the advantages which the engine itself may be made to afford.

INTRODUCTION TO PART II.

[IN this Part the Author proceeds to enter into the detail of his subject, and to investigate at considerable length the circumstances to be taken into consideration in the construction of the high-pressure engine; commencing with the boiler and its appurtenances, and the furnace.

The present *brochure* contains, *first*, the discussion of the boiler and boiler apparatus generally; and *secondly*, a minute description of the Author's first kind of boiler, used by him for small engines, together with its safety and feed apparatus, gauges, and other appendages.

The next publication will give an equally full description of another kind of boiler, suitable for larger engines, and a treatise on that most important but most neglected organ, the *Furnace*.

The most useful comment I can make upon these pages is to recommend them most cordially to all interested in the construction of steam engines, being fully convinced that, even although Engineers of equal authority with the Author may differ from him in some matters of opinion, there are few who may not benefit by his practical, experienced, and well-digested views.

A glance through the Table of Contents will show that much of the matter is applicable to engines of all descriptions, and not confined to those of high pressure.

I must again ask the reader's indulgence for any trifling errors which may from my absence remain uncorrected.

WILLIAM POLE.

Bombay, September, 1846.]

PART II.

ON THE BOILER AND ITS APPENDAGES: AND THE FURNACE.

44. I come now to my own high-pressure engines; to describe their peculiar construction; to explain the grounds upon which I have founded my choice of this construction; and to exhibit the plans I have adopted for generating and using high-pressure steam with economy. I shall endeavour to describe these machines and the apparatus belonging to them in as exact and complete a manner as possible; and shall also set forth their advantages with all the impartiality I can command.

When in London, I believe I made use, in my engines, of steam of a higher pressure than had ever been employed before. Once I worked an engine, for the sake of experiment, to a pressure of 1000 ℔s. on the square inch; and it was found that under this tremendous pressure, the engine itself remained perfectly firm and steam-tight in all its parts. On a subsequent examination, it appeared that the packing had become somewhat singed (*gebräunt*), and softer than usual;[1] nevertheless it retained the steam

---

[1] It is a general opinion that hemp packing is improper for a very high pressure, being destroyed by the great heat of the steam. When it is considered, however, that steam at the melting point of lead, at which temperature hemp is not destroyed, possesses an elasticity of nearly eighty atmospheres, the objection loses all force for such pressures as I have used.

perfectly well. This engine was constructed peculiarly for a very great pressure.

I firmly believe that these engines of great pressure would have produced useful results; but I conceived that the experience I had with them, was not based on sufficiently extended practice to determine a manufacturer in adopting them with security. The boilers, although they showed good results in experiment, were not perfected, and other generators for such a great elasticity were not at hand; nor would they, if procurable, have properly exemplified my plans of construction. Moreover, I had good grounds to fear that the public, already prejudiced against the high-pressure system, would oppose it so much the more as the steam used was of a higher elasticity than previously employed. Finally, I considered that to insure a proper care and attention to these engines would be a matter of greater difficulty than with those of a more moderate pressure; and that on this ground the convenience of their use would appear in some measure doubtful; and thereby an objection would be raised against them, which would require more time to remove than I had the opportunity of bestowing.

45. While, therefore, on these grounds I avoided the use of too great a pressure, I retained firmly the principle that the elasticity could not be reduced lower than eight or ten atmospheres, without relinquishing the advantages of the system. For—

(a.) The loss of the vacuum would be felt so much the more, the lower the pressure became.

(b.) The friction of the piston would be greater, by the use of a larger cylinder for the same power, and thus a greater prejudicial resistance would be sustained. Notwithstanding the improvements made in this part of the machine, the friction is still so great as to render it advisable not unnecessarily to increase its rubbing surface.

(c.) The engines would, at a lower pressure, be larger, less portable, and more expensive.

(d.) The principle of expansion could not be made use of to so great an extent, and to such advantage, with steam of a lower pressure. The steam leaving the cylinder would at the end of each stroke retain too little excess of pressure above the atmosphere, and therefore would blow out with too small a velocity, and leave behind an increased resistance to the piston. For example, steam of three atmospheres, expanded to three times its volume, would scarcely balance the atmosphere, and would thus have no tendency to blow out; while steam of two atmospheres similarly expanded, would sink so much under the atmospheric pressure, as to cause a very injurious counter-resistance to the piston from the entering air. Numerous experiments had convinced me of the great advantage of a rapid discharge of the steam from the working cylinder, and I resolved that this discharge must be at least effected with the elasticity of some atmospheres, to take place with proper rapidity, and produce the advantage I have before alluded to. It was also clear to me that the steam, before its departure from the cylinder, ought not to be so much reduced as to render the action too unequal, and thereby to require too large a fly-wheel.

46. In order to take a secure path in the fabrication of high-pressure engines, I conceived I could not do better than follow in the footsteps of Oliver Evans, and adopt as the normal for my future attempts, the pressure he had found to answer in his long and varied practice. Such a pressure had the advantage of allowing me to retain the use of several organs of the old engines, particularly the slide-valve, which presented peculiar advantages in use, and of whose superiority over the conical valve I was convinced by experience. Nevertheless with regard to the boilers of my engines, I strove to proceed upon more secure principles than Oliver Evans had done, and also to reduce the engine itself to a more simple and compendious construction and form, as well as to make its appearance more agreeable to the eye. I reduced the diameter of the boiler as much as I could without detriment to its evaporative power; and, in order to apply the power of the piston to the crank in the most secure and convenient manner and with the least loss, I gave the engine vibrating cylinders, in which last alteration I found it a difficult task to remove all the many defects consequent upon former arrangements of the kind. Fourteen years' experience has proved that I have succeeded in my endeavour to overcome the difficulties of my undertaking: daily have engines built upon these principles been working under my own observation; I have undertaken all necessary experiments and observations to enable me to decide accurately upon their advantages or disadvantages; and have spared no trouble, no exertion, no sacrifice, to improve their construction and make their results more perfect. Under all circumstances I have reduced the consumption of fuel, in comparison with low-

pressure engines, by at least one-third, often one-half, and sometimes still more; a result which points out as satisfactory the pressure I have adopted. The condenser I only make use of under certain circumstances, and give it then an entirely new and peculiar arrangement. I do not recommend any fixed normal form or arrangement of the engine, but, as I have already stated, I would vary the construction according to the circumstances under which the engines are required, and to suit the places where they are to be erected. Nevertheless a certain form may be taken as most preferable, and this I shall fully and particularly describe.

47. Many manufacturers and others skilled in the science of steam are yet of opinion that it is impracticable to work engines to such a high pressure as eight or ten atmospheres. They seem, however, to have forgotten, or not to have known, that such engines are already in use, and have been worked for a length of time with advantage, without requiring those many subsequent alterations and frequent repairs, or incurring the great wear and tear, that have been brought as objections against them. At the present time a great number of such engines are at work in America; in manufactories, in locomotives, and in steam vessels, particularly those upon the Mississippi and the Ohio. If any one with these facts before him still remain incredulous, let him come to me and examine my engines. He will see the simplicity, the steadiness, and the safety of their construction;—their smooth, noiseless, equable, and powerful motion;—and he may satisfy himself of the great amount of the work they are doing. He may

learn that their repairs only affect such parts as are common to all kinds of steam engines;—and that the attention and management requisite for them involve less application, trouble, and exertion, than engines of low pressure. His own observation will convince him that no greater quantity or intensity of firing is necessary for them, and that consequently their boilers are not more liable to deterioration.

48. In order to render the following portion of my work more clear and perspicuous, I shall treat separately of the several more important parts of the engine. Under each head I shall give introductory notices of the labours of previous inventors and improvers of the several parts; of the principles upon which they proceeded; of their errors; of the difficulties in the way of attaining perfection; of the requisites for a right treatment of the subject; and of the deductions I have drawn from my own experience, upon the best means of removing the difficulties and wants in the way. These will serve to introduce the details of the various improvements I have made.

THE BOILER.

49. The boiler involves more difficulty in its treatment than any other organ of the steam engine, particularly when used for high pressure. We have proof enough of this in the fact that no boilers exist which satisfy all the conditions required from them. That I do not here exaggerate, will be allowed by every one who has studied the history of the steam engine, or who has himself devoted his attention to its construction or use.

I have already entered upon the subject of the great defects of the old capacious boilers, and have shown that such apparatus, especially when they are of an angular, prismatic, or indeed any but a cylindrical form,—or even then if not made of wrought metal,—become the peculiar seat of danger in high-pressure engines. I have shown how all sorts of safety apparatus, as well for preventing too great a pressure, as for avoiding other sources of danger, are but uncertain in their operation, and not to be depended on while the objectionable form and size of the boiler itself remain; since so many fearful examples have shown that they are ineffectual in excluding danger, and are still more incapable of removing or mitigating it when it does arise.

50. And yet is this old monstrous form still used with great confidence; yet is it adopted by the great majority of engineers, and looked upon as the most suitable for the efficient generation of steam. All the frightful consequences of the explosions of vessels of this kind have failed in convincing those who employ them of their error; they have still followed the ancient track, and instead of striking at the root of the evil, have contented themselves with trusting, as their fathers did, to the superficial and imperfect safety arrangements so often relied on in vain. The many prizes and rewards offered. by academies and scientific societies for the improvement of safety apparatus, show plainly how the true great principle of improvement has been neglected, and the only secure method of avoiding danger overlooked. This great principle, this sure method, is, SO TO CONSTRUCT THE BOILER THAT ITS EXPLOSION MAY NOT

BE DANGEROUS.[2]　In all my researches and endeavours to improve the high-pressure boiler I have steadily kept this principle in view.

51. It is only lately that this condition has been somewhat approximated to by the invention and application of tubular boilers; but it would seem that these have been suggested rather by the necessity of providing, for many technical purposes, and particularly for steam carriages, boilers of less content and weight, than by the desire of removing or lessening danger from explosion.　Tubes have that form which is most adapted to resist pressure—viz., the cylindrical.　If then they are made of small diameter, of not too great thickness, and of suitable material, they may be made to carry out the before-named principle; *i.e.* they themselves, in case of their bursting, will not cause any dangerous consequences to the neighbouring persons or property.[3]　This is amply proved by experience.

Unfortunately, however, there are no tubular boilers which satisfy all conditions required.　We often hear the subject spoken of as one of little difficulty, easy of decision, and unencumbered with practical obstacles; but such is the language only of the prejudiced and the inexpe-

---

[2] "Die Kessel so zu construiren, dass sie selbst bei einer erfolgenden Explosion keine Gefahr verbreiten."　More literally, "So to construct the boilers, that they themselves, in case of an explosion ensuing, spread no danger."—TR.

[3] An instance is on record where the bursting of a connecting-pipe of scarcely 2 inches diameter, in a steamer, scalded to death in three minutes the engine attendant and two stokers, who could not escape from the engine-room in time.　It is a great fault in the construction of steam boats, that the engine and boiler-rooms are not separated from each other, and that the access to both is usually inconvenient.

rienced. To arrive at the truth, we must seek it with long-continued perseverance, and bring no small share of physical knowledge to our aid; for the subject is beset with perplexities on every side. It presents at every turn a thousand difficulties, a thousand dangers; and would we avoid a Scylla on the one hand, we find a Charybdis on the other. It becomes a most complex problem to construct a tubular boiler for a large supply of steam, by reason of the difficulty of arranging and connecting the great number of tubes it must contain, into one convenient whole. The modern English locomotive boilers cannot be legitimately called *tubular* boilers, because they fail altogether in the grand distinguishing quality of all such—namely, the small diameter of the generating apparatus. The tubes of these boilers are nothing more than a splitting up or sub-division of the ancient fire-tube of the Trevithick steam carriage boiler. From their great outer diameter, locomotive boilers do not avoid the evil of the old capacious form, and therefore do not diminish the objection to it. They have also a defect in the close proximity of the tubes to each other, whereby the water space between them is rendered too confined, and the heated tubes become liable to be laid bare of water. This circumstance gives the key to the well-known fact, that the tubes become so soon destroyed, or at least require constant repair, and to the mischief occasioned by their expansion, through their connection with the end plates of the cylindrical part of the boiler. It is evident that from the passage upwards of the steam formed among the lower tubes, the upper ones must be most liable to be uncovered with water; while these, being exposed to the hottest part of the fire current, are most likely to receive damage therefrom.

The new boiler of M. Neukranz,[4] which Mr. Penn, of Greenwich, usually adopts for steam vessels, is a better arrangement than that of the locomotives : in this, the tubes above the fire-place run across through the vertical fire channel in the interior of the boiler. These tubes are filled with water, have a greater diameter in proportion to their length, and embouche at both ends into the water space of the boiler. Unfortunately, however, these boilers, and all of similar construction, on account of their great circumference and content, are equally far removed from fulfilling the great object of the tubular system.

52. According to my opinion and experience, a tubular boiler ought to preserve, as much as possible, the tubular form in all its parts ; or, at least, the larger portions ought to be cylindrical, and not of too great diameter, or should be so strongly made that the tubes should form the weakest part of the whole boiler. The tubes themselves should be of such diameter, and be constructed of such metal, that in case of their actual bursting, no dangerous explosion may ensue. This, however, is only possible when their thickness is so small, and the metal of such a kind, that bursting takes place by a comparatively small internal pressure, and is followed by only a ripping open of the tube, and not a scattering about of massive fragments. Under all circumstances, however, the tubes must be the sole generating vessels ; they alone must receive the action of the fire, and be exposed to its destructive influence. All other and larger vessels, or parts connected with the tubes, should be most carefully protected from not only

[4] 'Gewerbblatt für Sachsen,' No. 49, p. 399.

this but all other dangerous influences, in order that they may remain in their original proved condition of strength.

Only such a tubular boiler as fulfils all these conditions can be called a safe one. In its use there is no further danger from high-pressure steam, and near it its owner may repose undisturbed by a care for the safety of life or property.

53. The requisites in the use of the tubes are the following :—They must be placed in such a position with regard to the furnace, that the flame may act upon them in the most favourable manner, and that the heat may be absorbed as completely as possible.—They must have such a proportion between their length and diameter, that neither the ebullition in them may become too violent, and the water be thereby ejected from them, nor that they be warped or made crooked by the heat.—They must properly convey away all the generated steam, and be regularly supplied with water.—They must be connected with the main part of the boiler in such a manner that in case of a rupture of one of them, the whole content of water and steam cannot suddenly and dangerously discharge itself.—They must lie so deep under the general water level of the boiler (in the receivers or separators) that some considerable sinking of the water may be allowed to take place without leaving any of them empty; and in case the latter effect should occur, such tubes must first be emptied as are least exposed to the heat of the furnace. Lastly, they must be connected with each other in such manner that no destructive expansion may be allowed to take place, and that all may be easily and conveniently cleansed of the earthy matters deposited in them.

The enumeration of such requisite conditions shows us the weight of the difficulties I have before alluded to. I will proceed to set forth these requisites still further.

54. The larger portions of the boiler, or receiving vessels, may themselves consist of tubes of a larger diameter, or may form flat chambers, constructed of a strength to withstand a very high pressure (say 400 to 500 ℔s. per square inch); this involves no difficulty.—The diameter of the receivers should not, where it can be avoided, exceed 16 inches, and they should be constructed of plate iron of at least ⅜ of an inch thick, securely and exactly riveted together into a cylindrical form.—When it is necessary that they should be capacious, their length should be increased and not their diameter beyond that specified, or their number should be greater.—Their covering lids (*schlussdeckel*) may be flat and of cast iron, but of considerable thickness (1½ to 2 inches), and these must be connected to the cylinders securely, and in such a way that they may be easily taken off when cleaning is required. —They must, under all circumstances, be entirely removed from all strong action of the fire, and must at most be exposed only to such currents as have discharged the greatest portion of their heat against the generating tubes.—In order to preserve them from rust, their internal and external surfaces may be covered with several coats of oil-varnish (*oelfirniss*), and the coating renewed, at least on the inside, every year.—Since these receivers or larger parts of the boiler usually serve as separators, and as means of connection between the generating tubes, they must be perfectly adapted to fulfil these purposes. As separators,

they must efficiently separate the steam from the water, so that none of the latter may penetrate into the working parts of the engine; and to this end the water surface in them must be of sufficient extent.—In order that the water may not rise to a dangerous height in them by violent ebullition in their tubes, their water space must bear a certain proportion to that of the tubes and the other parts of the boiler.—The steam room in them must also be proportioned to the content of the engine cylinder; so that the pressure may not be too much lessened by the discharge into the engine, and a foaming of the water thereby be caused.

55. The doctrine I hold that the tubes should form the weakest part of a tubular boiler, will, doubtless, at first sight appear to many of my readers a paradox, or at least a very hazardous rule, seeing that it is in the most glaring opposition to all former views on the subject, and sets all former theories on one side. But if the reasons I have to give in its favour be duly weighed, I trust it will be justified in the eyes of all discerning men.

When this arrangement is adopted, the place where an explosion becomes possible is confined to those parts whose bursting is unattended by danger, and the rupture will take place before the steam has acquired such an excessive elasticity as to produce any very violent effects. Those who have witnessed the bursting of thin copper tubes will bear me witness that by this arrangement all desirable extent of security may be attained. The tubes become safety-valves, whose functions are perfected when a pressure double or triple the proper one arises in the boiler, and when all other safety apparatus forsake their duty. Thin copper plates and sacks have heretofore been recommended and used for safety arrangements.

If it is objected that by the weakness of the tubes frequent accidents may occur, and that consequently the working of the machine may be often seriously impeded; I answer that a sufficient pressure to cause an explosion, even of these weakest parts, cannot frequently occur: it can only take place through the carelessness or wilful neglect of the machine attendant; and the ordinary safety apparatus are still at hand as far as they will succeed in preventing mischief. In one of my first engines, after many years' wear, the tubes became so much worn that ruptures were of frequent occurrence; yet these were attended with so little danger, that nothing was thought of them beyond the inconvenience of a few hours' stoppage of the engine for repair; and as I had a larger engine in course of erection, I did not think it worth while to renew the old boiler. If the tubes are so arranged, (as they were in my engine, and ought in all cases to be,) that a ruptured one can be replaced with facility and expedition, the objection I have alluded to loses all its weight. A boiler of this kind will possess thereby a great advantage over the common boiler, inasmuch as the latter, in case of explosion, not only is destructive to life and property, but also puts a stop, for a long period, to the work of the establishment. And to draw a parallel between the two cases, will any one assert that these old boilers, particularly for low-pressure engines, will bear a doubly or triply increased pressure with so little mischief as the rupture of one of my tubes would occasion? Is so sudden and dangerous an evaporation to be apprehended from thin tubes when they may accidentally become red-hot, and afterwards be suddenly covered with water, as from the thick sides of a large boiler? and would not the thereby suddenly increased pressure be more likely to confine its effects to the tube, connected only by a small opening to the larger parts of the boiler? Is not the drying and overheating of the tubes less likely to occur when the receivers or separators are arranged as I have before indicated? and particularly, is not such an occurrence less to be feared in a steam vessel exposed to the motion of the sea?

Tubes of small thickness have the advantage, that they generate more steam than surfaces of stouter metal; because the heat penetrates them more quickly. They are also not less durable, since the heat is less apt to accumulate and produce those destructive expansions and contractions to which, as I have before shown, thick boiler sides are so liable.

I have already stated that the larger receivers or separators connected with the tubes must not, if they are expected to retain their state of security, be acted upon by the strong heat of the fire, the effect of which must be expended upon the tubes, the least dangerous parts of the whole. One of the greatest difficulties in the construction of effective tubular boilers consists in the proper arrangement of the tubes in the furnace, and of the connections between these and the other portions of the boiler, with a view to the most perfect evaporation, and the most complete facility for the discharge of the steam and the supply of water.

56. The most common error in the construction of tubular boilers, is, that the diameter of the tubes is made

too small, and the length proportionately too great. This produces the following inconveniences.

(*a.*) The tubes present, for their length and breadth, too little surface to the fire; and therefore are required to be greater in number for a certain evaporative power.

(*b.*) Their connection becomes a matter of more difficulty.

(*c.*) They are more liable to be choked up with dirt and deposit, and when they become so, are more difficult to clean.

(*d.*) The discharge of steam from them is more apt to drive out the water and leave them dry, whereby they are exposed to speedy destruction by the fire.

(*e.*) By offering impediment to the free and equal flow of the steam and water, they are liable to become warped or crooked, and otherwise injured by an unequal action of the heat.

All these inconveniences are got rid of by giving the tubes a sufficiently large diameter; such as at least *four inches*. Tubes of this diameter are large enough to represent small boilers, which have a proper proportion of heating surface to their cubic content, and in which the water and steam space is so ample that the vapour may discharge itself without either carrying the water off with it, or at all hindering the proper supply. When tubes of such a diameter are made of suitable thickness of metal, no danger is to be apprehended from their bursting; for their steam and water content is of no considerable magnitude.

The length of such tubes may be *from sixteen to eighteen times their diameter*. To make them longer would render them liable to the objections I have alluded to, and to other inconveniences I shall hereafter explain.

A very important advantage of such tubes is the facility with which they may be cleaned. For this purpose they must be provided with suitable covers, capable of being removed with facility, to allow of the proper introduction of the cleaning instruments.

The connection of the tubes with the other portions of the boiler must be made secure, and in such a manner as to admit of their being easily renewed when requisite, and to prevent a sudden discharge of the whole contents in case of a rupture. The manner of accomplishing this, I shall show when I come to describe my own boilers.

57. The method of placing the tubes in the furnace so as to obtain the greatest effect of the fire, has been the subject of much difference of opinion; the modern view, however, is, as generally received, that a *vertical* position is the least advantageous. The heated current strikes upon vertical tubes and surfaces too swiftly, and finds too little resistance to enable it to discharge its proper amount of caloric.[5] If this is to be properly absorbed, the current must, in its draught through the furnace, strike as nearly as possible perpendicularly against the objects to be heated, and be so divided by them as to be compelled to vary its course. Many men of science have acknowledged this fact,[6] and experience on all sides corroborates it. How this may be done, I shall hereafter show. Suffice it here

---

[5] In one of my engines I adopted first the horizontal and afterwards the vertical arrangement; but although the latter had 50 per cent. more surface than the former, it required 50 per cent. more fuel.

[6] *Vide* 'Seguier, Recueil industriel,' 1831, pp. 1, 89, 155.

to say, that horizontal tubes are in this respect the more
suitable, as well as possessing all the other qualifications
of good evaporating vessels.   This position is, in many
respects, preferable to either the oblique or the vertical,
as my own long experience has amply proved.

So much for the conditions upon which tubular boilers
should be constructed: I shall have more opportunity of
exemplifying them further on.   Meanwhile, I proceed to
make some remarks upon tubular boilers in general.

58. Over-ebullition is least to be feared in tubes half
filled, since in them the steam space is well separated
from the water.   There is, however, much difficulty in so
arranging the supply of water, that when many tubes are
used together, it shall be kept at the same height in all. My
experience has shown me that this involves difficulties
even in tubes of large diameter, and produces evils which
are avoided by a different plan.   Half-filled tubes give less
evaporation than those entirely full, and therefore require,
for the same steam supply, the whole apparatus to be of
larger dimensions,—an objection often of great weight.
The disadvantageous ebullition above alluded to, to which
full tubes are more liable, is but little to be feared if the
tubes are constructed of proper dimensions, and are laid
in the furnace slightly on the incline, that the steam may
have liberty to escape freely by its levity, as it becomes
formed.

59. Many inventors of tubular boilers have recommended
a long coil of tube of small diameter running in many
windings through the furnace; receiving the water at its
lower end, and discharging the steam at its upper.   This

plan is objectionable, not only on account of the great difficulty or almost impossibility of cleaning the tube, but because variations in the intensity of the fire, or in the regularity of the feed, will inevitably produce a drying of some portion of the tube, and its consequent injury by the fire.

60. Tubular boilers are seldom used for low-pressure steam. They are more particularly adapted for high-pressure, in that the latter acquires a much smaller volume, and is generated with a proportionately much less violent ebullition. The higher the pressure, the smaller are the bubbles of vapour, and the easier their transmission through the water. Hence a tubular boiler that might, under a low pressure, fail from the drying of its tubes, answers perfectly well when the pressure under which it worked is increased. From this it follows that the pressure has a considerable influence not only over the ratio between the cubic contents of the tubes and the receivers and separators, but also upon the diameter of the tubes themselves, and the size of the openings by which they are connected.

61. When, after a fire is lighted under a high-pressure boiler, the water first begins to boil, the steam is formed under a low but constantly increasing pressure; and under such circumstances, the *volume* of the steam produced, and the consequent ebullition, are much greater than when the full pressure is attained. From the consideration of this we gather the rule, that caution should be employed in firing while getting up the steam, especially when the tubes are small, or the proportion between them and the

receivers unfavourable. If the fire is at first made too strong, the water will be driven out of the lower tubes, as will be evidenced by the rising and unsteadiness of the water level in the separators. When, however, the pressure has attained its proper height, the fire may be increased without fear, and the water will then resume its steady and accustomed level.

62. I have found that in the low-pressure boiler, the production of a cubit foot of steam per second requires a water surface of from 5 to 6 square feet, in order that it may be produced freely and without too violent ebullition: this supposes the steam to be evolved equally from every part of the surface. Here, therefore, is a *datum* for the proportions of the receivers of such tubular boilers as work with filled tubes; and we are compelled by this rule to give their water surface the greatest possible extent. Hence all upright receivers or separators whose length much exceeds their diameter, are objectionable, and on this ground many modern improvements on tubular boilers have failed. In steam vessels, however, the rule must be somewhat relaxed, as we have another element to take into consideration—namely, the motion of the ship, which has more influence on the level of the water in horizontal than in vertical separators.[7]

63. The great defect of almost all tubular boilers is the difficulty of cleaning them. This objection applies to

[7] The Author here proceeds to comment on the boilers of Gurney, Gillman, Ogle and Summers, Maceroni, Squire, Dance, Hancock, and others. I have not thought it necessary to insert these remarks, as the boilers alluded to are so little used in England.—Tr.

most of those boilers used for steam carriages on common roads, and all such inevitably contain the germ of their own destruction.

This most important requirement is always difficult to be accomplished in tubular boilers, and especially in those that contain a large heating surface with a small cubical content, since it is generally impossible to open them fully in order to gain convenient access to the interior surfaces. It has been therefore often attempted to effect the cleansing by chemical instead of mechanical means; and the attempt was at first taken up with great enthusiasm, owing to the satisfactory results which it appeared to afford. But it has been a delusion. I myself have given these chemical means a fair trial, and have found them not only expensive, but untrustworthy, especially the much praised application of muriatic acid (*salzsaüre*). I have found that the boiler-stone becomes thereby somewhat loosened, but never dissolved;[8] and I have always had afterwards to scrape off and remove it. If the diluted acid is allowed to work longer to effect the more perfect solution, danger is incurred of the metal becoming corroded, especially in those spots where no deposit may lie: this danger is most to be apprehended with iron boilers. It should be considered that the boiler's deposit consists not alone of lime, but of many other salts and substances, such as gypsum, &c., which resist the action of muriatic acid.

64. But little better success has attended the labours of those who have endeavoured, by means partly chemical,

---

[8] Den Kesselstein etwas erweicht, aber nie ganz aufgelöset.

partly mechanical, to *prevent the accumulation* of deposit in the boiler, and thus to render cleaning operations unnecessary.

One of the oldest of these means is the introduction of *potatoes* into the water. Upon the quantity necessary different views are entertained.[9] The action of this preventive is explained upon the supposition that the potatoes are converted by the boiling water into a slimy fluid (*brei*) which retains the precipitates finely suspended (as gumarabic suspends the pigments in water colours), and allows them to be removed with it; it being a necessary condition that the water be occasionally drawn off. I have used potatoes under my own observation for eight years in all imaginable ways ; sometimes in their natural state, sometimes peeled, and sometimes previously mashed into pulp; but I yet remain doubtful whether their use is attended with advantage or not. I have frequently found the deposit adhere as firmly with as without them, particularly in the connection tubes, where the ebullition has been considerable. It is so far certain, that where pure and soft feed water is at hand, their use is rather prejudicial than advantageous, as they tend to cause *priming*, and by passing into the engine render the hemp packings stiff and inelastic; besides which, they tend, especially when used whole and unpeeled, to block up narrow and confined parts of the boiler and its connections. In newly riveted vessels they may at first be useful in stopping small leaks in the joints, by gradually depositing and hardening therein. Also where the water is very hard or acidulated, potatoes may be of use in diminishing the destructive chemical

---

[9] According to Payen $\frac{2}{100}$ of the weight of water are introduced into the boiler.

action upon the metal. In these cases, or any others where advantage is thought to accrue from the plan, the potatoes should be peeled, in preference to using them in their natural state.

It has been asserted that the use of potatoes would loosen boiler-stone already hardened upon the plates ; but though I have taken great pains to prove the assertion by experiment, I have never succeeded. I at first imagined that the loose state in which I found the deposit in my boilers was owing to the application of this preventive; but, to my great satisfaction, I soon discovered that the result was produced as well without as with it, and since then I have never used potatoes where I could get soft feed water.

65. *Charcoal powder* has been recommended, but this, often renewed, would be expensive. *Clay* is also among the remedial substances named; but I cannot understand how the introduction of one earthy substance can prevent the deposit of another. Another method proposed to prevent the adherence of deposit is to cover the internal surface of the boiler with a coating of *black lead and tallow.* This, or indeed any oleaginous matter introduced into the boiler, is supposed to prevent the firm adherence of the deposit to its sides. *Grains of metal,* or *small balls,* are stated to act mechanically in keeping up a constant motion, and preventing the formation of hard deposit. *Troughs, separators,* and apparatus of various kinds, have also been introduced into boilers. And lately a patent has been obtained for an application of *vegetable matters,* such as dye-woods, turf, leaves of trees, &c., &c., for the same end. It has been also proposed to introduce certain *salts* in the feed water, whose acids will form easily soluble

compounds with the earthy bases of the deposits, or whose presence will otherwise prevent incrustation.[10]

66. Seldom, however, are any such preventives necessary for high-pressure engines. If the feed water is not very hard, a firmly incrusted deposit is but rarely found in their boilers. The earthy concretions generally collect in loose layers upon the bottom, or against the ends of the tubes: the layers consist usually of gravel-like masses, small and large pieces commingled, and they may be easily removed with a scraper. When the tubes are small, this must be frequently done; otherwise stoppages may be produced in the water passages. For this purpose I have so constructed my boilers that they may be most conveniently opened and cleaned from time to time. If it is wished still more to prevent the accumulation of this loose deposit, I recommend half a bucket of water to be drawn off occasionally, during the working of the boiler, when the water is at its highest level. This plan has the double advantage, that not only a great mass of the deposit in formation is blown off, but the water is prevented from attaining that state of saturation in which the hard precipitation begins. Where muddy or slimy, or salt water is used, this frequent blowing off is especially necessary.[11] In my boilers the draw-off opening is situated as low as possible, and I find all the impurities and salts which collect at the bottom of the boiler are thereby easily removed.

[10] I have abbreviated this paragraph, since the Author's remarks upon these methods contain no information of importance. References to all his authorities are given in the original.—Tr.

[11] Messrs. Maudslay and Field's brine pumps act on this principle.

67. Although the amount of evaporation depends on the extent of the heating surface of the boiler, through which the heat of the fire is applied to the water; and although on this account a vessel with a small *water content* may be made to evaporate as great a quantity of water as one in which the same element is large, provided the amount of heating surface is the same in both;—yet it is a great mistake to reduce the cubic content of the vessel to the extent many inventors have done, imagining such an alteration to be advantageous. A small water content has indeed the good property of enabling the steam to be raised at first with a reduced loss of time and fuel; but it has a more important disadvantage in making the action of the boiler too irregular, and too much dependent on changes in the amount of the load on the engine, or in the intensity of the fire; besides rendering a greater degree of care and attention necessary in the management. I will explain this more at length.

When a boiler is first set in action, the water gradually rises to the boiling point, and then begins to evolve steam of atmospheric pressure. The firing being continued, the vapour, unable to escape, begins to collect in the steam chamber, acquiring constantly a greater pressure and density; and the water assumes an increase of temperature corresponding to the density of the steam; for otherwise the evaporating process could not continue. The converse of this takes place when the pressure and temperature of the steam are reduced. I have before remarked that when the pressure upon the water in the boiler is lowered, a portion of the free caloric in the water will be employed to form steam; and this takes place whenever, by either an increased consumption of steam in the engine, or a reduced firing, the pressure in the boiler is lessened: evaporation will then continue till the temperature of the water assumes that corresponding with the pressure of the steam. Now the evaporation thus produced will be the more rapid, and last the longer, the greater the quantity of water in the boiler; and this water content thus tends to act as a provision against a too sudden diminution of pressure by a relaxed firing. On the other hand, the same provision also prevents too sudden an increase of pressure when the fire is increased; since steam of a higher elasticity cannot be generated before the whole volume of water has acquired the corresponding temperature; and this requires a longer time in proportion as the volume is greater. Thus boilers with a large water content work, for these reasons, much more regularly, even with a less regular firing; and the greater the volume, the greater the regularity. We must not, however, be led, on this account, always to give the greatest content possible, but must, as in so many other matters, adopt the golden mean between the extremes of irregularity on the one hand, and unnecessary waste of time, fuel, and material on the other.

This mean is better arrived at by experience than by complicated calculations. In my own practice I have adopted the rule, founded on my own experiment and observation, that for every *eight* or *ten square feet* of heating surface, there should be allowed *one cubic foot* of water content. This rule is to be observed even in tubular boilers with small tubes, if they are provided with receivers or separators. How little this practice has been followed in the majority of tubular boilers, must be too obvious to need demonstration.

68. Of equal importance with the consideration of the water content of a boiler, is that of its *steam space*. It is wonderful to observe how contradictory are the rules laid down for guidance on this point. But since contradictory rules are useless, I pass them entirely over, and turn again to my own experience. High-pressure engines have on this head a great advantage over low-pressure, especially if they are worked expansively. They have a much less volume of cylinder to be filled, and since the steam space must bear a direct proportion to this, a less space is required for a given power as the pressure is greater and the steam used more expansively.

The following considerations should lead us to a just determination of the proportion between the two.

(*a.*) The steam space should be so large, that in the discharge from the boiler to the cylinder, the pressure in the former should not fall in any considerable degree, and the mercury in the manometer steam gauge should not exhibit any considerable fluctuation. I find this condition is fulfilled under all circumstances in my engines when the cubic content of the steam space is at a minimum *twenty* times as great as the space to be filled with steam in the cylinder. If it can be made greater, consistently with the other arrangements of the boiler, so much the better.

(*b.*) The steam space should be capacious enough to prevent the danger of *priming*. The water in the boiler has always a tendency to rise immediately under the steam opening when the discharge takes place and the pressure is diminished; but I have found that the proportion of space I have above mentioned is sufficient to prevent this, especially if due care is taken that the steam opening is sufficiently elevated above the water level, and is situate over that portion of the water where the least ebullition is likely to take place; for instance, as far as possible removed from the *débouchements* of the tubes.

How few of the modern tubular boilers conform to these requirements! [12]

69. The present will be the most convenient place for introducing an investigation of the question,—what amount of heated surface (*feuerberührungsfläche*) is necessary for a certain power?

On no point connected with steam engines has there been more error than on this. It is most remarkable to see the strange views which have been held respecting the sources of the evaporative power of the boiler, and, among these, one of the strangest is the idea that this power depends upon the water content or the water surface, irrespective of the amount of surface exposed to the fire. Rules based on these erroneous principles will be found in many English works on the steam engine. But the dimensions and proportions of high-pressure boilers seem to have been altogether involved in confusion. It has been imagined that because the engines themselves, or their cylinders, have been of less magnitude than for low-pressure engines of equal power, therefore the size of the boilers might also be proportionately diminished, and a less amount of heating surface might suffice. Thus we often find only about *five* square feet per horse-power

[12] The Author here, in the original, is very severe, and not without reason, upon the many fallacies published in England, some of them in an authoritative dress, upon this point.—Tr.

allowed in such engines, and sometimes indeed less than this. Now although it is quite true that a high-pressure engine does require a less volume of steam in proportion to its effect, yet it by no means follows that the heating surface is to sustain the same proportionate diminution. If it *is* so diminished, no wonder that it is found requisite to increase immoderately the size of the furnace, and thus to introduce the most monstrous disproportion between this and the dimensions of the boiler. I have frequently seen one foot of fire allowed to four of heating surface; and have never met with an instance where a correct proportion was maintained. Errors of this kind are remedied by forcing the intensity of the fire, but this always involves a greater expenditure of fuel, and an increased wear and tear of the boiler and furnace. Is it possible that fuel can be economized under such circumstances? Is it not evident that the boiler and furnace-bars must under such a use be sooner destroyed than in low-pressure engines? And are not these errors thereby the cause of bringing the high-pressure system into unmerited obloquy?

And yet is the matter so simple, its treatment so obvious. In order that a certain quantity of heat may be taken up, a certain amount of surface must be exposed; and this must be so much the greater, the *less* the difference between the temperatures of the boiler and the fire current. But this difference is obviously less in the high-pressure than in the low-pressure boiler, and therefore the former would appear to require a *larger* surface for a given power than the latter.[13] Since, however, according to experiment, an equal heating surface,

[13] *Watt* allowed for his low-pressure engines 8 square feet to evaporate 1 cubic foot of water in one hour, producing one horse-power. But by far

acted upon by an equal fire, will produce an equal amount of evaporation at all pressures, we obtain a rule that the fire surface should at least be equal at all pressures, for an equal quantity of water evaporated.

When the surface is so arranged that the greatest possible amount of heat is abstracted by the boiler, this should be testified by the temperature of the current which escapes into the chimney being reduced to nearly that of the boiler; and the more the former exceeds the latter, so much the farther are the arrangements from perfection, and the greater the loss of heat and fuel.[14]

70. The following are the rules I have been led to by my experience and researches:

(*a.*) High-pressure boilers should have much greater surface exposed to the heated current than hitherto generally given them. For high as well as low pressures the allowance should be—

For small engines of from *one* to *six* horse-power, 14 square feet per horse-power;

---

the majority of low-pressure engines require 1½ to 2 cubic feet, and therefore Watt's rule agrees tolerably well with the one I have given further on. This great man followed always the path of experience,—the only direct road to knowledge; his active life was spent not in calculations but in the work of his laboratory. WATT appeared as a dazzling meteor whose brilliant ray illumined the darkness of his age. But his light is extinguished, and since his time its place has only been supplied by the dim tapers of his followers and imitators, whose dulness seems rather to recall the ancient darkness than to perpetuate or renew the splendour which his great spirit threw upon the world.

[We beg to take an exception here in favour of the Cornish men.—TR.]

[14] It is possible to make the smoke current pass off into the chimney at a temperature even lower than that of the steam in the boiler, and I believe this is common in Cornwall. See 'Treatise on the Cornish Engine,' Art. 130. —TR.

From *six* to *twenty-five* horse-power, 12 feet per horse-power; and

From *twenty-five upwards*, 10 feet per horse-power.

With these proportions a less surface of *fire-grate* than usual will suffice. I allow

In engines *under twenty-five* horse-power, 1 square foot of grate for 14 feet of heated surface;

In larger engines, 1 square foot to 16.

Under these proportions I find that no more heat escapes into the chimney than is necessary to produce a moderate draught; the fuel is economized; and undue wear and tear prevented.

(*b.*) The surfaces should be so placed in the furnace that the heated currents may be made, as much as possible, to impinge perpendicularly upon them. The heat is by this plan most quickly and completely absorbed, but it is not always free from difficulty in its application. The most advantageous arrangement is when the current strikes upwards in a zigzag direction among the tubes of a tubular boiler; so that after it has passed through the narrow spaces between the lowest range of tubes, it impinges upon the tubes themselves in the second range, placed immediately over the spaces in the former; and so on among the whole. The current is thus divided into thin sheets, whose heat is much more readily abstracted than in the large flues of the common boiler, where only the external part of the current is brought into immediate contact with the surfaces to be heated. The plan I have here recommended will be fully illustrated in the second form of boiler I shall hereafter more minutely describe.

71. Many improvers of boilers have tried means of increasing the evaporative power without giving a greater extent of heating surface; by introducing into the boiler pebbles, shavings, saw-dust, brass wire, shot, &c. I have found some of these actually increase the evaporation, in a degree generally depending on their conducting power. The heat appears to pass easily from the heated surfaces of the boiler to the loose metallic bodies, and to be distributed thus over an increased surface to the water.[15]

72. I have now another question to consider which is of the greatest importance with high-pressure boilers—namely, how great their diameter should be. On this point also there is much error existing. We constantly find a diameter of 5 or 6 feet given to vessels intended to bear a pressure of 4 or 5 atmospheres; indeed a less diameter than 3 or 4 feet we seldom meet with; under 2 feet, never.

Many rules exist for calculating the diameter and thickness of metal of boilers of various construction and material;[16] but these do not touch the principal question,—

[15] Mr. Williams, of Liverpool, has lately taken out a patent for a new method of increasing the transmission of heat to vessels containing water or other fluids, by inserting metallic pegs or conductors through the portions of the vessel acted on by the fire; thus increasing the surface both inwardly and outwardly. I had at an earlier date attempted something similar, but found that the oxydation on the outside, and the deposit on the inside, frustrated all my attempts.

[This invention, embodied however in a more comprehensive claim, forms the subject of a patent taken out about eight or ten years ago by Mr. John Sylvester, of London.—Tr.]

[16] One of the best treatises on this subject is that by Professor Johnson, of the Franklin Institute. It may be found in the 'Repertory of Patent Inventions,' January, 1832, p. 44. The formulæ seem, however, to me imperfect,

how far we may increase the diameter consistently with safety. Nor indeed are such formulæ necessary if we limit our boilers to a certain size, or confine them to a given diameter in all cases. Further, such rules are to a certain extent mischievous, in that many manufacturers may trust too implicitly to them, and fall into a dangerous confidence which may subsequently prove entirely misplaced. If we determine to retain the same size of vessel for all cases, the dimensions and thickness will be soon found by experience, without any great amount of trouble.

According to my views, a satisfactory degree of safety may be obtained in two ways. Either

(*a.*) By making the diameter as small and the thickness as *great* as possible; whereby the vessel is enabled to withstand a pressure very much greater than usual, and to remain secure even after considerable wear: or,

(*b.*) By giving the vessel a small diameter, and only a *small* thickess of metal; such a thickness as will not allow the pressure to increase to too great a degree, and will in case of rupture spread the least possible danger.

Experience alone can lead to a proper decision on this point. I shall hereafter describe two kinds of high-pressure boilers, both of which I have used with perfect success, and whose perfect safety has been practically proved. In the first, used for small engines only, I do not allow the diameter of the tubes (both are tubular boilers) to exceed 12 inches. It consists of two ranges of tubes, the upper 12 inches and the lower 8 inches diameter, and I find a thickness of ¼ inch amply strong

---

inasmuch as they are calculated by the strength of *bar* iron, whereas the *plate* iron of boilers is generally so much inferior in cohesive strength.

enough, whether the material be iron or copper: the latter being a weaker metal, would theoretically require a greater thickness than iron, but I find this, or even $\frac{3}{16}$ of an inch enough. I have proved that such plate will tear open without danger. In three instances, copper vessels of this construction have burst without doing the least damage; and in one of these cases I was standing opposite the fire-door and looking into the furnace at the time the accident occurred, but I did not receive the slightest injury.[17] Oliver Evans made the diameter of his cylindrical boilers 2 feet, and their thickness 2 lines: they seldom produced any mischief, but simply opened in rents which caused no damage. It would be well worth investigation whether, even for boilers of large diameter, thin metal is not less dangerous than thick. There appears every probability that the former would produce nothing but a harmless rent, where the latter would cause a most destructive explosion, scattering fragments in every direc-

---

[17] This was with an engine of ten horse-power, erected by me at a paper manufactory at Bützow. I was called in by the foreman, on account of the engine having begun to slacken its speed. I found nothing the matter with the engine itself, but turned to the boiler, and immediately perceived that the float had considerably sunk. I quickly opened the fire-door, to check the combustion; and as I looked into the furnace to examine the intensity of the fire, the explosion took place. It was accompanied with a dull report in the furnace. A portion of the fuel and some steam and water crackled (*prasselten*) around me, but without hurting me; and after an examination I found a rent 2 feet long, and in one place 6 inches wide, in one of the lower tubes. Notwithstanding this explosion, not a stone of the furnace was displaced, not even in the thin division wall between the tubes.

Both the other explosions I have named were equally harmless. One was in a large, the other in a small tube. Both were caused by a deficiency of water, and in both instances the fire-door was shut. In the first case a few stones were displaced, but with so little force that they were not removed a couple of paces from their original position.

tion. For copper vessels, I would adopt the thin metal without hesitation.

In my second form of boiler, I have adopted thin copper tubes which alone are exposed to the action of the fire, upon the principle already stated; viz., that they may form the weakest part of the whole boiler; and therefore, if a rupture takes place, it can only happen in the tubes, from which, on account of the tenacity of their material and their small diameter, no danger can arise. It must not be forgotten that the thinner the tubes are made, the more quickly they transmit the heat from the fire to the water they contain.[18]

73. The question, what metal is most suitable for the construction of boilers, is almost answered already. Copper is in every respect the best material, not only on account of its extraordinary tenacity, which prevents its flying in pieces, but also because it is a better conductor of heat than iron. It is dear, costing nearly five times as much as iron; but when old it may be disposed of advantageously, and will generally realize at least half its original price.

When fuel is used which evolves acids of sulphur in the combustion, as is the case with many kinds of turf and pit coal, copper is more affected than iron: the former is, however, less susceptible of injury from rust, and upon the whole may be pronounced the more durable of the two. For steam navigation copper is much to be preferred, as it is less injured by the action of sea water. An iron boiler under such circumstances seldom lasts

---

[18] Thick metal, however, tends, by storing up heat, to *regulate* the action of irregular firing, like a large water content. See Art. 67.

longer than four years, while a copper one will endure seven, without requiring removal from the vessel for any extensive repair.[19] With fresh water an iron boiler will last usually seven years. Iron is, as already remarked, more cohesive and firm (*haltbar und fest*) than copper, but does not retain its toughness so long; it flies in pieces, and does much mischief on explosion.

Other metals than these two are seldom used for boilers, except for some detached apparatus; such as gun-metal (*messing*) for valves, cocks, floats, &c. This metal has also of late been used for the small tubes of the Stephenson locomotive engine, as more durable than copper. It also expands more equably with the iron of the boiler, and is therefore less likely to produce derangement of the connections.

Copper tubes have the great advantage that they may be joined with hard solder (*schlageloth*). Joints so made, if properly done, are not only much more likely to be tight than riveted ones, but are usually firmer and more tenacious than the substance of the metal itself. In cases where my copper boilers burst I have always found the soldered parts undamaged, whereas iron boilers always give way at the riveted joints, these being the weakest parts of the whole. This is evident, since the rivet-holes remove a large part of the metal; and the closer the rivets are placed, the weaker the boiler becomes. Many boiler-makers adopt a double row of rivets, placing them wider apart, and the rivets in one row opposite the spaces in another. Whether this plan is attended with advantage I cannot say, not having the warrant of experience

---

[19] *Vide* the evidence of Mr. Joshua Field, on the question of steam navigation to India.—'Mechanic's Magazine,' No. 620, p. 249.

for decision.   Of my boilers, only iron ones of the first described kind are riveted; these are done in the simple manner, but with the greatest care.

It has been asserted that copper, when used in combination with iron in the construction of steam boilers, induces a galvanic action destructive in some degree to both metals, but particularly to the iron.[20]   I have, however, constantly used both in combination in my boilers, but have not found this effect to ensue.   It is indeed very difficult to construct copper boilers without using some iron in conjunction with them, particularly for bolts and fastenings, for which copper or brass would be too weak to make the joints perfect and durable.   But when has it ever been found that in the engines themselves, where several metals, such as iron, copper, brass, tin, and lead, have been used together, that any such destructive galvanic action has ensued?   And yet in many of these cases the parts have been equally exposed to the combined action of heat and moisture.[21]

74. I now come to treat of the *appendages to the boiler.* And first of

THE FEEDING APPARATUS.

In modern times the opinion has considerably gained ground, that explosions of boilers seldom occur in consequence of a gradual increase of elasticity of the steam. On the contrary, unequivocal proofs have been presented

---

[20] Janvier on Steam Vessels and their Engines.

[21] The Author after this inserts a short passage on *boilers of injection:* this I have not thought it necessary to copy.   Such boilers are scarcely known among English engineers.—Tr.

in many cases that the accident has been preceded by a diminution instead of an increase of elasticity. Now in the great majority by far of such instances, it has been found that this was accompanied by a sinking of the water level below its proper line. I have in a former part of my work treated of this occurrence as one of the probable causes of explosion; but without reference to this, the undoubted fact that such a sinking has frequently accompanied accidents of this nature, is sufficient to induce the necessity of great attention being paid to the perfection, in principle, manufacture, and action, of the apparatus for the supply of water.

Unfortunately, however, it must be admitted that the complaints we so commonly hear of the untrustworthiness of apparatus of this kind, especially in high-pressure engines, are not without ground; for many of the machines ordinarily constructed for supplying boilers are very imperfect, and in their use entail constant danger of failure. Much ingenuity has been expended on this object,[22] but yet with little success. The improvement of the feeding apparatus is attended with much more difficulty than appears at first sight; but it seems to me that this difficulty is much enhanced when attempts are made to get rid of the old apparatus, the *pump*, and to substitute new contrivances in its room; for all such, as experience has shown, involve more defects in themselves that are inherent in the machine they are intended to supersede.

75. Almost all substitutes for the feed-pump depend on

---

[22] Here the author refers to the descriptions of apparatus by Hall, Franklin, Jeaks, Potter, Taylor, Pequeur and Hallette, William, Baddeley, White, Fox, Seguier, Pott, Taylor and Davis, Whitelaw, and others.

one principle, the only variations being in the mode of its application. A chamber is put in communication alternately with a water reservoir and with the steam boiler. From the former it fills itself with water, and when this communication is interrupted and that with the boiler opened, the contents are allowed to flow into the boiler. The entrance of the water into the chamber is effected partly by its gravity and partly by the condensation of the steam which finds its way into the chamber from the boiler when the water is discharged. Many of these apparatus have been so arranged that they would only fill the boiler to a certain height, namely, the prescribed water line, the action of the apparatus ceasing spontaneously when this level is attained.

The opening and closing of the communications to the chamber are usually effected by means of cocks. In many instances, the whole depends upon a single one, which contains the chamber in itself, and by its motion presents its opening alternately to the passage from the water vessel and to that from the boiler.

All these apparatus have, however, been attended with but little success, and as often as new improvers have attempted to revive them, so often have they again fallen into oblivion. One principal cause of this failure is, that the cocks and rubbing apparatus employed to change the motion have soon become deranged by the deposit from the water, and the variations of temperature to which they have been exposed. This derangement would of course be greater in proportion as the rubbing surface was more extensive; and on this account those machines which enclosed the chamber within themselves have usually most disappointed the hopes of their patrons.

76. The force-pump hitherto commonly in use has in every respect the advantage over all these contrivances, if we leave out of view the expenditure of power, sometimes not inconsiderable, necessary to work it. When, however, a proper construction is adopted, which will enable the action of the pump to be relied on, its simplicity and convenience will always much outweigh any objection that can be brought against it on the ground of its consumption of power. But hitherto most of these force-pumps have been far from perfect. Among the defects most common, I may name especially a faulty construction of the plunger and its stuffing-boxes, or of the piston, cylinder, valves, &c., &c. For example, the plunger may be badly turned and not exactly cylindrical, and the stuffing-boxes too large and badly packed; or the cylinder may be carelessly and unequally bored, and the piston imperfectly leathered,—so that air will enter and destroy the efficiency and regularity of the action. Or the openings may be so situated that air which has once entered cannot be again expelled. Or the valves may be faulty in many ways:—they may not be made of the proper metal (gunmetal, *messing*), but of some other which will soon oxydate;—they may be too heavy, so as not to open with sufficient ease;—they may be imperfectly and improperly fitted to their seats;—they may give too little opening;—they may be badly guided, and be liable to fall improperly back upon their seats;—their stalks may be too short, or may shake in their guides, or may be liable to wedge and stick fast, or to be easily fixed by impurities in the water;—their surfaces of contact may be too broad, or too narrow, or too conical;—they may be unprovided with proper arrangements for withdrawing them for repair or cleaning

when they become leaky or foul; for these pumps require a constant watchfulness, and all their parts should be easy and convenient of access when derangement is observed. If these defects exist, it may be safely asserted that the pumps will often fail in their duty, and will require a great expenditure of time and trouble to put them in order again, thereby causing the most inconvenient and dangerous interruptions in the action of the engine to which they are attached.

To the before-named imperfections we may add others; such as an improper height of the suction-pipe, preventing the entrance of the water in sufficient quantity under the plunger, especially when warm water is used for the feed, by which vapour may be generated and the vacuum necessary for the action of the pump destroyed. Or the strainer may be too wide in the mesh, whereby impurities may find their way inside;—or too narrow, so as to be soon stopped up;—or it may be improperly placed, so that the impurities of the water may collect against it. Or the air-cock, which is often attached to the pump to discharge any air that may have entered, (and which by the before-mentioned faulty position of the openings may not be able to find its way out otherwise,) may be productive of more evil than good, by admitting air instead of discharging it. These cocks, so inconvenient to manage, ought never to be wanted, if the pump is properly made.

Again, apart from defects in the construction of the pump, many other causes may arise to obstruct or interrupt its free action: such as faults of the attendant, in not bestowing proper care on the state of the apparatus, or in neglecting to purify the water from straws, chips, sand, or the other endless varieties of dirt which may be liable to accumulate therein. Or the locality may be unfavourable to cleanliness, as in cement-works, gas-works, grinderies, saw-mills, &c. Or the water itself may be naturally bad, containing impurities of a mechanical or chemical nature that may have a deteriorating effect upon the working of the pump or the state of repair of its various parts. Against such evils as these nothing but care and continual watchfulness can provide a remedy.

THE SAFETY APPARATUS.

77. Safety-valves are also often of very defective construction. One of the principal faults is the face of contact (*dichtungsfläche*) being made too broad. This has the great disadvantage, that when the valve is opened, the steam, penetrating between the conical faces of the valve and its seat, acts upon a considerably larger surface than when closed; and as a consequence the valve, once opened, will not shut again till the pressure is diminished below the elasticity which opened it, and which is supposed to be the normal pressure. I have frequently remarked that under such circumstances the elasticity has been diminished upwards of two atmospheres before the valve closed: the use of a good manometer will show the fact.

Another fault frequently found in the construction of safety-valves is making them of iron. Such valves rust easily, and stick fast, as I have often witnessed in England.[22] Gun-metal valves are not indeed entirely free from this danger, but are much less liable to it than iron ones. It is to be recommended that all valves should occasionally be lifted from their seats, and their state examined. This

---

[22] *Vide* 'Mechanic's Magazine,' No. 862.

precaution would render the use of two valves to one boiler unnecessary; an arrangement often recommended, but seldom found to be of much practical utility; for the reason that the one which is usually locked up is neglected, and soon becomes useless.[24]

78. The cause of the sticking of safety-valves often appears enveloped in mystery. Frequently this accident occurs in consequence of the presence of some substances in the water, which, being driven through the valve, become adhesive on drying. I have very often observed sticking take place immediately after a too wide opening of the valve with the hand, whereby generally some water has been discharged with the steam; and this has particularly happened when the water in the boiler has contained potatoes, clay, or mud. Many wonderful and incredible stories have been related in reference to the sticking of valves, and much more wonderful and incredible hypotheses have been invented to explain them; but in most cases, were the exact circumstances more accurately known, they would be found to be much less extraordinary, and capable of much more simple explanation than has been supposed.

The invention of the safety-valve was one of the most important of any connected with the steam engine. It has been claimed by the English, but is generally attributed to Papin. Whether he was actually the inventor does not appear to be made out with exactitude; but it cannot be controverted that he was the first who made use of high-pressure steam, and that the first mention of the safety-valve is made among the records of the inventions he left behind.[25]

[24] *Vide* 'Cornish Engine,' Art. 143.
[25] I have omitted a disrespectful sneer at English appropriation of inven-

79. The conical safety-valve with lever and weight appears to me the best suited for the high-pressure engine, especially if it is so arranged that the weight may be fastened in its place by a set-screw. The use of a spring, as adopted generally on locomotives, does not seem advisable. If it is of steel, it easily rusts and fails in its action; and if of brass, is liable in some measure to the same defect. Both lose in elastic power by heat, and cannot then be depended upon.

It has been objected to conical valves that they do not long remain steam-tight, but require very frequently to be re-turned and ground; but I have not observed this even under the highest pressures, and conjecture that such an effect must have been caused by other circumstances. Or perhaps valves with flat seats may have been referred to. These ought never to be used, for they are not only proved by experience to be more liable to stick, but they require a larger ground face than conical valves, and are subject to other and greater objections.

---

tions. I am not aware that our historians have laid claim to the invention of the safety-valve. Other exceptions might easily be taken to the paragraph in the text.

Weighted valves or plugs opening upwards were used before Papin's time for the purpose of allowing vapour enclosed in a vessel to escape when its pressure increased beyond a certain amount. Some of the ancient steam deities were thus fitted, and apparatus of this description are noticed by Estienne and Lebault, 1574; Glauber, before 1650; and French, 1651. "Papin's claim, therefore, is not to the valve itself, but to its improvements, or rather to the mode of applying it by means of a lever and moveable weight (proposed by him in 1681 for his digester); thereby not only preventing the valve from being blown entirely out of its place, but regulating the pressure at will, and rendering the device of universal application." He did for the safety-valve what Watt did for the steam engine itself, namely, extended and generalized its use; and as long as the safety-valve shall be used, the world will be his debtor. *Vide* Ewbank on Hydraulic Machines.—Tr.

80. I have already spoken in another place of several kinds of safety apparatus, such as fusible plugs, warning bells, sacks, &c., and multitudes of contrivances for the same object may be found recorded.[26]   I will only mention that all such as allow the escape of steam when the water level falls, appear to me obviously attended with more danger than they pretend to provide against.

The French *Société d'Encouragement pour l'Industrie Nationale* have, for a long time past, offered a prize for a perfectly satisfactory arrangement for the prevention of explosion of steam boilers.   The invention, however, of such an arrangement would pre-suppose an exact knowledge of all the causes of boiler explosions, from which we are unfortunately at present far removed, since almost all we can say on the subject rests upon bare hypothesis alone. We have already seen that regulations for preventing the undue increase of pressure are, alone, insufficient to provide against danger.   Undoubtedly the Society would have acted more wisely had they offered a reward for a boiler whose explosion should be unattended with disastrous effects : they would then have laid the axe to the root of the evil, and the state of our knowledge in regard to the causes of explosion would have been but of little matter. With a boiler fulfilling this condition, we may contentedly trust to our ordinary safety arrangements, especially if we take the precaution to secure engine attendants of good character.   Such men, when they fulful their duty in a careful and intelligent manner, afford more security than all the most ingeniously contrived apparatus.   If they are ordinarily gifted with the power of observation, they may

[26] The Author gives some references in a note.—Tr.

easily interpret all the appearances which present themselves in the working of the machine, and, aided by a
manometer, may deduce therefrom the constant state of
the evaporative process. The important requisite is, that
the attendant must thoroughly understand and take an
interest in his machine; must constantly strive to bring
it to the greatest possible degree of perfection; and must
take his greatest pleasure and pride not only in increasing
its effect, but in maintaining the perfect cleanliness and
repair of its individual parts, and the beauty of its external appearance generally. The praise of his engine
ought to inspirit him; while its detraction should be to
him a source of discomfort.[27] Men of this class can, however, only be retained by those proprietors who themselves take an interest in their engines, and personally
show a good example to their inferiors by devoting their
own attention to the care and improvement of their
machinery.

81. Safety-valves with pistons are sometimes used. A
packed piston, weighted for a certain pressure, slides in a
cylinder which has a gradual enlargement at its upper end.
The piston-rod passes upwards through a guide, and carries
the weight. When the steam rises beyond a certain
pressure, the piston passes into the enlargement of the
cylinder, and the steam finds room to escape round it.

[27] I have noticed with true pleasure the extraordinary interest which an
engine attendant in England always feels for his engine. It is his joy, his
pride. He rejoices when it is praised, and treats those who find fault with it
with pity and contempt. This warm and lively interest generally tends considerably to the exaggeration of the character of the machine, on which
account we can but seldom place much trust in the statements of engine
attendants as to the useful effect or the consumption of fuel.

The variable state of the packing must, however, produce uncertainty in the action of this apparatus.

82. Thermometers are only of use as safety apparatus when they act quickly, and when their indications are frequently compared with those of other gauges. By themselves they are neither true indicators of the elasticity in the boiler (since low-pressure steam may be overcharged with caloric), nor are they to be trusted for giving warning of other dangers. In my opinion, they may well be dispensed with, being very fragile, and requiring great care in their fixing and management.

PRESSURE GAUGES.

83. Among arrangements for facilitating the control of the pressure in the boilers of high-pressure engines, may be named principally the manometer, an instrument well known. After once proved, it is eminently trustworthy, and becomes indispensable to the engine attendant in regulating his firing according to the varying pressure of the steam in the boiler. In high-pressure engines the ordinary mercury gauge used for low pressure cannot be employed, as the mercury column would be required inconveniently long. This is to be regretted; for this apparatus is undoubtedly more simple and secure, and less liable to derangement than the manometer, which has the evil, that in case of a vacuum being accidentally formed in the boiler, the air above the mercury is so apt to escape. The only way to prevent this danger is either to shut off the communication between the boiler and the manometer by a cock while the engine is standing, or to provide the boiler with a vacuum-valve.

Gauges for steam pressure on the principle of the spring steelyard have often been recommended. Upon an instrument of this description is fixed a small piston, working steam-tight in a cylinder exposed to the pressure of the steam. The more the pressure increases, the higher rises the piston, and the resistance of the spring, increasing in like ratio, is indicated by an index pointer. But it is impossible to expect exactitude in an instrument of this description, where the variable friction of the piston must so much influence the correctness of the indications.

WATER GAUGES AND REGULATORS.

84. The apparatus for ascertaining and regulating the height of the water in the boiler is of the greatest importance. According to the present state of our knowledge, we believe by far the majority of explosions to have resulted from the water level in the boiler having sunk too low, and therefore the indication of this level cannot be too secure and exact.

A host of arrangements have been proposed for this object, and among these the common *gauge-cocks* are perhaps the most imperfect of all. They ought most especially to be banished from low-pressure engines, although they are almost universally used for these, especially in England. But in no case do they give any certain indication of the height of the water in the boiler. When, for example, the lower cock is opened, the water which issues tends to evaporate instantaneously into steam by the reduction of pressure, and it becomes difficult to tell whether water or steam is observed. And when the upper gauge is opened, the water level in the immediate neighbourhood of the internal aperture of the pipe rises so much (in accordance with a well-known result whenever a current of steam is issuing from a boiler) as often to deliver water with the steam, to a considerable extent, even although the general water level in the boiler may stand at its proper and normal line.[28] Moreover, there are other evils attending the use of these gauge-cocks. The steam or water discharged endangers the observers, besides being the source of much dirt and deleterious moisture in the boiler and engine-rooms. The inconvenience of manipulation of these cocks, compared with others which require but a single glance to read their indication, also point them out as much inferior.

85. Besides gauge-cocks, water gauges are reduced to two kinds; viz., floats and glass tubes, both which are too well known to need description.   Both have their advantages and defects. The defects of the float are its sluggishness and want of sensibility;—of the glass tube, its liability to fracture, and to the loss of its transparency after long use.[29] Glass tubes are moreover uncertain in their action, from the liability of their connections with the boiler to be stopped up by dirt in the water. These connections are frequently furnished with cocks, which it is said might be

---

[28] See the researches of the American Boiler Commission. 'Mechanic's Magazine,' No. 666, &c.   See also 'Cornish Engine,' Art. 148 : 'Repertory of Patent Inventions,' Sept. 1832, p. 186 : 'Bulletin de la Soc. pour l'ind. nat.,' June, 1840, p. 197.

[29] M. Meier, of Mulhausen, has protected the tubes upon locomotive boilers by an exterior additional glass tube, which also shields them from the access of cold air. He has also contrived a simple arrangement for preserving their transparency. These improvements, however, render the apparatus complicated and expensive. See 'Bulletin de la Soc. ind. de Mulhausen,' No. 57.

closed in case of the fracture of the tube; but it seems to me that after such an accident it would be next to impossible to get at them in the midst of the scalding discharge which would ensue.

86. Floats are simpler instruments than glass tubes, and if their defects are removed, are not much exposed to accident. I have in my practice found them always the best and most certain indicators, since I have succeeded in improving their construction. On the old plan, the floats hang on thick wires or rods, which pass out of the boiler through stuffing-boxes, and are attached to one end of a lever whose other end supports a weight of sufficient magnitude to keep the stone floating. This arrangement, however, hinders the motion and free play of the machine: the thick wires, especially if of iron, soon become oxydated, and cause great friction in the stuffing-boxes, which the floats do not possess sufficient force to overcome, since this force is only derived from the difference of specific gravity between the float and the water; or at least they must be of great magnitude in order to act with the sensibility necessary for tubular boilers, where the water receivers are small. I shall hereafter show my improved construction of these floats.

The material of which the floats are made is very important. At first I tried hollow copper bodies, but I found these frequently collapsed, for I could not make the copper sheet strong enough without intrenching too much on their power of flotation. Such floats are also too light and moveable, and, following even the slightest movements in the water, keep in a state of continual oscillation which much detracts from their value as indicators. A good

H

float should not vary by such slight movements in the boiler, but should remain steady at the line of water level. Stones fulfil this condition best, and they are therefore much preferable to hollow bodies. Of course a part of their gravity must always be balanced by a counter-weight.

87. In my high-pressure engines I have altogether abandoned the plan of regulating the water level or supply to the boilers by any self-acting apparatus. I have found by experience that such arrangements soon become defective and useless, most of them being out of the reach of observation; and when so, they place the boiler in a much worse and more dangerous position than without them.— If floats act upon regulating cocks or valves, these latter soon stick or otherwise get out of order, either through the changes of temperature and the action of the water, or on account of the deposition of earthy matter within them. But the worst of all such apparatus is, that they give the boiler attendants a dangerous idea of security, and tend to make them careless of their duty, and to prevent them bestowing proper attention upon the height of the water in the boilers and the condition of the feeding apparatus. I have always found that in order to make these persons watchful and careful, their duty must not be made too easy and convenient for them. If they know that the water level in the boiler regulates itself, they will trouble themselves little about the feed apparatus at all; but if they have constantly to watch the varying height of the gauges, and thereby to regulate the admission of the water, they are kept in a salutary and intellectual state of activity which prevents them from becoming mere machines, or working by mere instinct like the lower animals. The

caution of the attendants is by this means also extended to the state of the pump and the whole feeding apparatus; and should any defect in the supply be apparent, the cause may be immediately discovered, and a remedy applied before any dangerous consequences arise.[30]

ON THE PROVING OF BOILERS.

88. I will say a few words on this head before I proceed to describe my own improvements.

The general impression is, that a boiler is perfectly secure if proved by hydraulic pressure, before being used, to three times the elasticity of the steam it is destined to contain; and much reliance is placed on this test, especially for high-pressure boilers. For my own part I must honestly declare that I have not participated in this opinion; for I am convinced that a boiler when heated is not to be considered in the same condition as regards strength, as when cold; and that consequently a trial made in the latter state affords no security for the former. If boilers are made of given small diameters, and their strength proportioned to withstand a six or eight-fold pressure,—if they are constructed on correct principles, and above all things in such a manner that an explosion will not entail any considerable danger,—the process of proving is quite unnecessary, and does more harm than good, inasmuch as it tends to expose the metal to an over-straining which may afterwards produce dangerous rents and leaks when the heat comes to be applied. Besides, this process only provides against such dangers as ensue from a gradual increase of the pressure of the steam, and not

---

[30] *Vide* Pole on the Cornish Engine, Art. 147.

against those much more common ones arising from sudden accidents, such as the overheating of the plates and subsequent flow of water upon them. The Government regulations adopted in many countries with regard to steam engines and their boilers are often immature and unpractical, as may well be believed when we consider that they mostly originate with persons who know the steam engine only by what they hear or read of it. It appears to me that there are no means of proving the tenacity of boilers before used, which shall be perfectly satisfactory and suited to the subsequent conditions of their working. The only security is to be found in the character of the manufacturer for uprightness, conscientiousness, ability, talent for and experience in his calling; and in the skill and honesty of those who work under him. And after the machine has left his hands, the responsibility of keeping it in its pristine state of safety lies upon the user, to whose order, care, and interest it is confided. If Government regulations are to be provided at all, they should be directed more against the engine attendant than the engine builder. This would be to hit the right nail on the head; for in this respect much is and ever will be wanting while temptations to intemperance and dissipation for people of this stamp exist and multiply.

DESCRIPTION OF THE AUTHOR'S IMPROVED BOILERS.

89. Having now, in these remarks upon high-pressure boilers and their apparatus generally, endeavoured to lay before the reader the true principles from which scientific and advantageous improvement should spring, I proceed to describe my own arrangements. My readers may thus be better enabled to judge how far these deserve to be called

improvements, and to appreciate the motives which have led me to adopt them.

I have already remarked that I make use of two kinds of boilers for my high-pressure engines. The first kind serves particularly for small engines of from one to ten horses' power, the second for those of a larger size. Both are tubular boilers, and each shall be described in its turn as exactly and fully as possible.

I. DESCRIPTION OF THE BOILER FOR SMALL ENGINES.

90. This first kind of boiler consists of tubes or cylinders of large diameter, which I construct of plate iron or copper. Of these cylinders I take a greater or less number, and make them of various lengths and diameters, according to the power required and the circumstances of the case; but I never let them exceed one foot[31] in diameter. I always arrange them in two rows, one upper and one lower, and the lower ones are the smallest in diameter. The thickness of every cylinder bears a constant ratio to its diameter; and I use the following proportions for both iron and copper:

For 12 inches diameter, the thickness is $\frac{1}{4}$ inch.

,, 8 or 9 ,, ,, $\frac{3}{16}$,,

,, 6 ,, ,, $\frac{1}{8}$,,

---

[31] The measure used by the Author in his drawings, and referred to in his text, is the *Hamburgh foot* (Hamburger fuss), which, like our own, is divided into 12 inches (zoll), each subdivided into eighths. This measure is shorter than ours in the ratio of about 15 to 16; but for the sake of simplicity I have allowed the stated dimensions to remain the same in the translation as in the original; and for all practical purposes they may be considered as English measure.

The true length of the Hamburgh foot is

One upper and one lower cylinder together will be called *a pair*.[32]

In fig. 3, such a pair is shown as fixed in the furnace, the latter being represented in a vertical section : *a* is the upper, *b* the lower cylinder.

The two cylinders of each pair are connected with each other by a short vertical tube (*c*), situate either at the front or back end,—the front the best.   This tube is usually 10 inches long. Its size is dependent upon that of the boiler. If the latter is 12 feet long, the connecting tube should be 4 inches diameter; if 8 feet long, 3 inches ; and for small boilers of 6 feet long, it should be at least 2½ inches diameter in the clear.

The ends of all the cylinders, both upper and lower, are closed with strong cast iron covers : these may be adapted to only one end, but the operation of cleaning is much facilitated if both ends are so provided.

The lower cylinders (*b*) are quite filled with water; the upper ones (*a*) only half filled, the upper half of these cylinders forming the steam space.   See fig. 4, where three pairs of cylinders (*a b*, *c d*, and *e f*,) are shown in vertical section; *a*, *c*, and *e*, referring to the steam spaces

---

0·28642 French metres.

or 0·9397 English feet.

or 11·2764 English inches.

A Hamburgh ell contains two Hamburgh feet, or 0·6264 English yards. See Scherer's ' Allgemeine Contorist,' article *Hamburg*.

The above table will suffice if it is desired to reduce any of the dimensions in this work to their true English equivalents.   Or, multiply the Hamburgh dimensions by 31, and divide by 33; the result will be the equivalent in English measure.—TR.

[32] *Eine lage*. I know of no term equivalent to the original, which would answer in this case. I have therefore substituted the one in the text. *Layer* and *tier* give the idea of a horizontal position.—TR.

in the upper cylinders. The steam spaces of all the cylinders are connected with each other by rising connecting tubes. (fig. 5, *g, h, i*) which open into a common steam pipe (*k*), lying across the boiler. The water spaces are united by similar tubes (fig. 6, *l, m, n*), proceeding horizontally from the lower part of the covers of the lower cylinders, and opening into a common tube (*o*).

Upon the steam-pipe (*k*) are fixed one or two safety-valves (figs. 3 and 5, *p*), and the index (figs. 1, *p*, and 5, *q*) of the float that shows the water level in the boiler. Upon the connecting tube (*o*) of the water spaces is a draw-off cock (fig. 6, *r*).

The connecting tubes leading to the steam-pipe (fig. 5, *k*) I place as far as possible from the tubes (*c*) which connect the upper and lower cylinders together, in order to prevent the ebullition from the latter carrying water into the steam-pipe and to the engine.

The float also should be as far removed from these latter named tubes as possible, that it may act in still water, and not be subject to disturbance from the ebullition.

The cylinders being open to each other, the water stands at exactly the same level in all. Any disturbance of this level should be participated in as quickly as possible by the whole boiler, and for this reason the water connecting tubes (fig. 6, *l, m, n, o*) should not be too small; for large boilers 2 inches, for small ones $1\frac{1}{2}$ inch diameter in the clear, will suffice.

91. When the cylinders are of iron, I construct them of plates riveted together; but when of copper, I join the sheets with hard solder. The connecting tubes are riveted to the cylinders in all cases.

The riveting of iron cylinders is performed in the ordinary way, but with the greatest care, so that the joints may be perfectly sound. This is the more necessary since high-pressure steam is an exceedingly subtile fluid, and finds its way through the smallest crevices. I use only one row of rivets, and these I drive in the usual manner, *i. e.* red-hot. The rivet-heads I make strong and of large diameter, and the riveted ends I spread out by a stamp to a good extent in a hemispherical form. In this·manner they are made to cover well the spaces between the rivets, and when they contract by cooling, they thus compress the plates more perfectly together. In order that the rivet-holes may attain the utmost regularity of form and position, I *bore* them in preference to punching them. I am then enabled, before the operation, to adjust the edges together, which much simplifies the process, and compensates in some degree for the extra trouble. The more exactly the rivet-holes are arranged, the more perfectly are they filled by the rivets, and the better the joint when finished. For plates $\frac{1}{4}$ inch thick, I make the rivets $\frac{5}{8}$ inch in diameter, and set them $1\frac{1}{2}$ inch apart, measured from centre to centre.

92. But notwithstanding the greatest care, riveted iron vessels seldom prove perfectly tight. In order therefore to make them so, and to fit them for holding high-pressure steam, I adopt various contrivances. If the leaks are few and small, I fill the boiler with water, empty it again, having marked the defective places, and let it remain one or two days empty. The leaks then rust up more or less perfectly, and if small, usually become tight; if not after the first operation, at least after its being three or four

times repeated. But if more important leaks remain, I besmear the joints or rivet-heads with the well-known iron cement (a compound of iron filings, sal-ammoniac, and flowers of sulphur, mixed up with water to the consistence of a paste),[33] taking care not to use it in such quantity as to corrode the metal to an injurious extent, and applying it where possible *inside*, that the pressure may rather tend to drive it into the crevices than out of them.

Iron cement is far preferable to any other material for making iron joints. It has the excellent property, that it becomes more sound and tight the longer it stands, so that cemented joints which at first may be a little leaky, soon become perfectly tight.

There is but little ground to fear for the soundness of a well-riveted iron boiler, for in time the action of rust and deposit will stop almost any crevices. In order however to take all precaution, it is to be recommended that some clammy substance, such as horse-dung, bran, coarse meal, or potatoes, should be boiled in the vessel before it is

---

[33] The following is the best way of preparing this iron cement. Take 16 parts of iron filings, free from rust; 3 parts powdered sal-ammoniac [muriate of ammonia]; and 2 parts of flowers of sulphur: mix all together intimately, and preserve the compound in a stoppered vessel kept in a dry place, until it is wanted for use. Then take one part of the mixture, add it to 12 parts of clean iron filings, and mix this new compound with so much water as will bring it to the consistence of a paste (*dicker brei*, thick pap], having previously added to the water a few drops of sulphuric acid.

Instead of filings of hammered iron, filings, turnings or borings of cast iron may be used; but it must be remarked, that a cement made entirely of cast iron is not so tenacious and firm as if of wrought iron; it sooner crumbles and breaks away. It is better to add a certain quantity, at least one-third, of the latter to the former.

If leaks to be stopped with cement are very large, it may be economized by adding clean river sand, but not to the extent of more than a fourth of the whole mass.

used: a very small quantity also of the same kind of substance may be put into the boiler when first set to work. This will find its way into the crevices by the pressure within, and, gradually hardening, will soon render the vessel perfectly sound.

By these means I have always succeeded in rendering my iron-riveted boilers perfectly steam and water-tight, even for the highest pressure; and I have been much astonished at hearing the complaints of others on this point.

Copper cylinders, if they are well soldered, remain perfectly tight as long as they last, and none of the beforementioned precautions are necessary with them.

93. In order to fasten the covers upon the ends of the cylinders, whether copper or iron, I rivet upon each end a ring 2 or $2\frac{1}{2}$ inches wide and $\frac{3}{8}$ inch thick, placing the rivets in two rows, those of each row alternating in position. The rivets of the second row from the end (in the upper cylinders 12 or 14, in the lower 8 or 10 in number) are provided with projecting cylindrical heads, $\frac{3}{4}$ inch diameter, and projecting 1 inch: upon these fit the eyes of $\frac{3}{4}$-inch screw eye-bolts, which pass through corresponding holes in the cover, and serve to fasten it against the cylinder end. The cast iron cover is 1 inch thick, and has a strong iron projection cast upon it which fits into the interior of the cylinder. The edge of the cylinder abutting against the cover is fitted with great exactness, and turned if possible; and a corresponding groove is turned in the cover, into which the end of the cylinder accurately fits. A ring of pure soft lead is introduced into this groove, and the joint is thus made tight between the two surfaces. This circular groove in the cover is indispensable,

that the ring of lead may not flatten out when compressed.

I make use of this arrangement, viz., the turned projection and corresponding groove, in all cases where I use lead for the joint, and can strongly recommend it wherever sound and durable joints are required. When lead is introduced between bare surfaces, it is always necessary to turn upon them narrow but deep grooves, into which the lead may be pressed when screwed up, so as to avoid lateral extension.

The arrangements just described are shown on an enlarged scale in figs. 7 and 8. The former is an external view, the latter a section: a is the cover; b and c are eye-bolts, and $d, d, d,$ the cylindrical projecting rivet-heads, upon which they hold: $e\,e$ is the projection on the cover which fits into the cylinder; $f\!f$ is the groove into which the turned end of the cylinder enters, and in which the lead ring is held; $g\,g$ is the ring riveted, by the rivets (d and h), upon the end of the cylinder.

In order to give still greater security to the covers and to the cylinders themselves in the direction of their length, when of larger diameter, a strong bolt, with a head at one end and a screw and nut at the other, may be passed through both covers, running the whole length of the cylinder. This, however, interferes with the float, and is not necessary for cylinders which do not exceed 12 inches in diameter.

As I have already stated, it is not absolutely necessary that both ends of the cylinders should have loose covers. In many cases, especially with short cylinders, convenient for riveting, one end may be of strong iron plate, riveted on. These ends should, if possible, be hammered into a spherical shape. I must, however, again observe that the process of cleaning is much facilitated when both ends can be made to open; a consideration of great weight.

94. The water-tube (fig. 6, *o*) connecting the lower cylinders with each other, I generally make of copper. It is best situated outside the back end of the furnace. Into this tube open as many small connecting pieces (fig. 6, *l, m, n*) as there are pairs of cylinders. They are furnished with strong iron flanches soldered [brazed] on, by which they are screwed to the cylinder covers, the joints being made tight by interposing the *double cones*, hereafter described. One end of the junction tube is furnished with a draw-off cock, for emptying the boilers; the other end is stopped with a blank flanch, unless it is preferred to introduce the feed water by this aperture. In order that the boiler may be completely emptied when the draw-off cock is used, the pipe (*o*) must be connected to the cylinders at their lowest level, as otherwise water would remain within them. For the same reason this connection is best made at the back end of the cylinders, because they are fixed so as to incline a little downwards towards that end.

This pipe and its connections are very apt to be encrusted with the deposit formed in the boilers, and it is therefore necessary they should occasionally be removed and cleaned, a very easy operation if constructed as I have described.

I have in most cases introduced the feed water into this junction tube, for the reason that it would be thus distributed most regularly among all the vessels: but more recently I have found that by this arrangement not only is the tube more exposed to the deposit of boiler-stone, but that this deposit distributes itself also into all the cylinders, which is not the case when the water is introduced into only one vessel, and that the upper one of the pair. Since the boiler-stone, and especially the carbonate of lime, its prevailing ingredient, first begins to precipitate at the time when, and in the vessels where, ebullition commences, it has a tendency, under the latter named arrangement, to deposit itself, as I have experienced, in the upper vessel alone. It is superfluous to show how much simpler, easier, and shorter this must render the process of cleaning.

95. The connecting tubes between the upper and lower cylinders are made of cast iron when iron cylinders are used. They are of adequate strength, the metal $\frac{3}{4}$ inch thick, and have a strong flanch cast on each end, curved to fit the upper and lower cylinders respectively. The joints are secured with six screw-bolts, $\frac{5}{8}$ inch diameter, to each flanch, and made tight with iron cement laid in as thin a layer as possible between the flanches and the cylinders.

For copper cylinders I make the connecting pipes in two pieces, screwed together in the middle by two strong wrought iron flanches, soldered on to the copper tubes. The joints I have best made of copper rings, of $\frac{1}{4}$-inch copper wire soldered together, whose upper and under surfaces were filed to a sharp edge projecting in the middle. The crowns of these connecting tubes are made of copper, and riveted to the cylinders. I have found this arrangement very suitable to the purpose, and perfectly strong and tight.

In figs. 9, 10, and 11, the connecting tubes are shown on a magnified scale. Figs. 10 and 11 show an elevation and section of the cast iron ones: *a* and *b* in both figures are the flanches, whereby they are fixed to the cylinders. Fig. 9 shows the tubes as made of copper, and connected to copper cylinders: *a* and *b* are the crowns, riveted to the cylinders, *c* and *d* are the flanches between which the copper joint-ring lies. This ring is drawn separately in figs. 17 and 18, which show the sharp filed edges. These sharp edges adapt themselves accurately to the flanches, and form a most secure and durable joint.

96. The steam collecting pipe (fig. 5, *k*) which lies above and across the whole boiler, and is connected to the upper cylinders, is, for iron boilers, made of cast iron. It is in as many pieces as there are pairs of cylinders. Each piece consists of an upper horizontal part (1) and a lower descending branch (2) at right angles to the former, giving the whole the form of a T. All three ends of this piece are furnished with flanches, that on the descending branch (3) being curved to fit the upper cylinder, and the two others (4) serving to connect the various pieces with each other. When thus connected, the two outside flanches of the whole may be used for attaching the pipes to convey the steam away to the engine or elsewhere, as may be required. The steam-pipe (5) leading to the engine is always made of copper and polished. The other end (6) may be used to convey steam to any other apparatus, or to the manometer, &c.; or may be closed with a blank flanch.

Two of the pieces of which the steam collecting pipe

is made must have an additional ascending branch, opposite the descending one, and giving the piece the form
of a cross. One of these carries the safety-valve, the
other the index of the float. In figs. 1 and 3, both
these are shown; in the latter (at p) the safety-valve,
in the former the float index, the tubes in front of this
being supposed to be removed. The whole of the joints
of the before-mentioned flanches are made with iron
cement.

In copper boilers, all these tubes and pieces are of
copper, with strong gun-metal or wrought iron (the latter
the better) flanches. The flanches are soldered on, and
have projections and corresponding grooves to hold lead
jointing, (which is best cut from sheet lead,) as before
described. Or else they are fitted for the double cone
joint. The descending branches (fig. 5; 2, 2, 2,) are
riveted tight upon the upper cylinders. When gun-metal
flanches are used, I slip them upon the tubes and turn
up the edges of the tubes over them. These edges then
form small flanches of themselves, which I solder with
soft solder to the gun-metal flanches. When two flanches
thus constructed are put together, the small flanches, or
ends of the tubes, abut upon each other, while the large
gun-metal flanches serve to receive the screw-bolts which
hold the joint together. The joint may be made tight
by the previously described copper ring, or by the double
cone.

97. I will now proceed to describe this beautiful arrangement, the double cone joint. It consists of a short
tube, a little smaller in diameter than the tubes to be connected, and whose external surface is turned into the form

of a double cone,[34] or rather of frustra of two cones placed base to base. The ends of the main tubes are bored out, or ground upon a rounded and polished mandrel, so as to fit upon the cones, taking care, however, not to reduce too much the thickness of metal. The cone is placed between these, and the flanches screwed up, when the conical surfaces adapt themselves closely to the bored ends of the main tubes, and render the joint perfectly tight and sound.

The double cone joint is shown in fig. 15 in section: *a* and *b* are the ends of the pipes to be joined, and *c* is the double cone, a view of which is given in fig. 16. Its surfaces are slightly curved, which renders the junction more sound and durable: *d* and *e*, fig. 15, are the flanches of the tubes to be joined, and *f* and *g* two of the screw-bolts which hold them together and press them upon the cone.

This double cone joint is the best that can be made for high-pressure steam. It forms a perfectly tight closure, even for an enormous pressure, and always remains secure and trustworthy. The cones seem to be the best when made of iron, especially if the metal is soft and of good quality. The joint closes best when the edges of the tubes are somewhat sharp. Copper cones are softer than iron, and may therefore be used when the screws are not too powerful.

The double cone joint appears to have been first mentioned by Jacob Perkins, who deserves great thanks for this beautiful invention.

[34] I adopt the Author's use of the term *cone*, although not quite correct, as the surfaces are afterwards said to be slightly *curved* in the direction of their length.—TR.

It is evident that the opening or canal in the cone must be proportioned to the quantity of fluid passing through ·it. If it is wished to make the joint without diminishing the passage way, the flanches must be bored out deeper, to receive the cone. This arrangement is exhibited in fig. 15.

98. I allow a greater area to the horizontal steam collecting pipe, than to the pipe which conveys the steam to the engine. The latter, in high-pressure engines, is often made too large. I have found that for 150 square feet of heating surface of boiler, with steam of 8 atmospheres, 3 square inches clear area of steam-pipe is sufficient; or one-fifth of the diameter of the cylinder is ample. The loss by friction of elastic fluids moving in small tubes has been much over-estimated, and is really of but little consequence. I give to the horizontal steam collecting pipe double the area of the pipe leading to the engine; because the steam has in this to make angular motions which tend to interrupt its course and diminish its velocity.

99. The *safety-valve* I use is a conical valve with a three-cornered stalk, whose three surfaces are grooved out to increase the steam way. The conical faces are at an angle of 45 degrees with the axis, and are as narrow as possible for the reason stated in Art. 77. The lever is arranged in the ordinary way, and the weight acts upon the valve through a short rod jointed to the lever, and pressing by a blunt end upon an indentation made in the valve. Care must be taken that this short rod bears vertically upon the axis of the valve, that it may not press it on one side, and so cause undue friction or imperfect closing.

I

Fig. 12 shows such a valve, with its lever and weight, in elevation; and fig. 13 the valve and seat, in section: *a* is the upper part of one of the pieces of the steam collecting pipe; *b* the valve, *c* the support for the fulcrum of the lever; *d* the lever, with its weight *e*; and *f* the short rod which presses on the valve. Fig. 24 is a horizontal section of the pipe and valve-stalk, showing the three rounded sides of the latter.[35]

The valve, as well as its seat, must always be made of hard gun-metal; the lever, its support, and rod, may be of iron. The lever must be made to move very easily in its fulcrum. The joint must occasionally be oiled to prevent it from rusting, for the escaping steam tends to oxydate all these parts. The lever must be provided with deep notches in which the weight may hang free from risk of sliding: these notches should be so arranged as to give increments of pressure of 10 ℔s. per square inch on the valve, and the pressure corresponding to each should be engraved upon the lever.

The diameter of the safety-valve, or rather that of the pipe on which it is placed, I make equal to that of the steam-pipe leading to the engine. Too large valves have the disadvantage of requiring unwieldy weights and clumsy apparatus, and are really unnecessary. When it is considered that at 8 atmospheres' pressure, an opening of at most ¼ inch diameter will emit as much steam as can be generated by 100 square feet of heating surface, favourably situated over a lively fire; we have no occasion to fear that the dimensions above prescribed, even although the

[35] There is some confusion in the Author's first plate, which I have endeavoured to rectify. The figure last mentioned is omitted altogether. —TR.

space is somewhat contracted by the valve-stalk, are too small.[36]

100. For a *water gauge*, I prefer, as I have already remarked, floats to all other arrangements. I believe that these, as I construct them, are free from the defects of apparatus of the kind as formerly used; at least I have found them by long experience in the highest degree accurate, sensitive, durable, and trustworthy, when carefully managed.

Fig. 14 shows this float arrangement. Inside the boiler swings a double-armed lever (*a*), its frulcrum (*b*) being supported by a bracket (*c*) screwed to the boiler. The motion of the lever must be free and unimpeded. On the long arm is fixed a conical-shaped stone, 8 inches long, and 4 inches in diameter at one end, tapering to 3 inches at the other. This may be made of firm sandstone, or else moulded and burnt in good brick. It has a hole in its axis which is fitted upon the lever; one end of the stone abutting against a collar (*e*) and the other being fixed by a nut (*f*). On the shorter arm of the lever (*a*) is fixed a cast iron or lead counter-weight (*g*), of such weight as will retain the stone floating with half its mass immersed. The long arm is so bent that the fulcrum (*b*)

---

[36] M. Köchlin gives (' Bull. de la Soc. de Mulhausen,' No. 48,) the following formula for the diameter of the safety-valve:

$$d = 2 \cdot 6 \sqrt{\frac{c}{n - 0 \cdot 412}}$$

where *d* is the required diameter, *c* the heating surface of the boiler in square metres, and *n* the number of atmospheres' pressure.

The Prussian regulations for steam engines enact, that the area of the opening of the safety-valve shall be $\frac{1}{3000}$ of the total heating surface of the boiler. For high-pressure engines a much smaller area will suffice.

and the short arm of the lever always remain above water, as seen in the figure. If a tension-rod passes through the centre of the cylinder, (see Art. 93,) the float must be double, *i. e.* there must be one on each side the rod. In order to give the stone more cohesive strength, I wrap it round with fine brass wire, taking care on the one hand that the meshes are not too small, and on the other that the weight is not too much increased.

The short arm of the lever carries a hook (h), in which is linked a brass wire (i) of $\frac{1}{16}$ inch diameter: this passes up one of the head pieces of the steam collecting pipe (l), and through a stuffing-box (m) into the outer air, where it is fastened upon the short arm of another lever (n). This lever swings upon a prop (o), and carries on its long end an index to show the height of the water in the boiler. The proportions between the arms of the two levers are so arranged that the index of the outer one moves through the same space as the centre of the float-stone; or, which is the same thing, as the water level. In order that the friction of the vertical connecting wire may be easily overcome in its upward as well as its down-ward motion, a small weight (g), easily adjusted by experi-ment, is hung upon the long end of the lever. The friction is, however, so trifling, that the motion is suffi-ciently free, and shows the water level in all its changes. The stuffing-box requires but little packing to make it tight, and the rod is durable and easily renewed when worn. In short, I can recommend this arrangement as one of the most secure, trustworthy, and suitable to its purpose, that can be devised. It is obvious that it must exceed in sensibility the ordinary float arrangement, since the wire (i), whose friction in the stuffing-box (m) is the obstacle to motion, is so much nearer to the fulcrum than in the latter.[37]

101. The following *general remarks* apply to my first description of boiler.

I place this boiler in the furnace in such a manner that the heat of the fire strikes first against the lower cylinders, which, being full of water, may receive the fire current on their whole surface. The current flows parallel to the tubes, and passes upwards between them at the back part of the furnace, returning then towards the front along the upper range of cylinders. Now, since these latter are only half filled with water, their upper half must be covered and protected from the fire current. This arrangement is clearly seen in fig. 5, a vertical section of the boiler and furnace. The generation of steam is most rapid in the lowest tubes, which are exposed to the first action of the fire; and as these are so arranged that the back ends lie lower than the front, where they are connected with the upper cylinders, the vapour generated easily escapes into the latter through the connecting tubes. It may carry, however, some little water with it, which will cause the water level at first to rise somewhat in the upper tubes; but this effect soon ceases when the pressure increases, and the steam assumes a smaller volume. When the evaporation first commences, slight crackling shocks may be heard in the boiler, arising from the condensation of the bubbles of steam first formed, by their meeting with cooler water in their course.

[37] The joint *b* may cause trouble: the Author does not show how this is provided against.—TR.

The passage of the steam from the lower to the upper cylinders usually takes place interruptedly. This may be known from the gurgling noise, which resembles that made by water rushing out of a hole in a cask to which the air cannot gain access. The water must return in a certain quantity from the upper to the lower cylinders, to supply the place of that evaporated, and thus an effect is produced analogous to pouring liquid out of a narrow-necked bottle.

It will be easily understood that a strong ebullition takes place in the upper cylinders immediately over the pipes which open into them from the lower, and it is therefore advisable not to place either the steam-pipes or the float near this situation; they should be as far removed as possible, where the level of the water is less disturbed. If this precaution is attended to, there is little reason to fear either priming or the undue oscillation of the water index.

It is easy to perceive that through the means of the connecting pipes (fig. 5, *k*, and fig. 6, *o*), the steam and water chambers in all the pairs of cylinders are made common, and the steam and water distribute themselves thereby equally among all, even though the heat may often vary in different parts of the furnace. The boiler thus fulfils the difficult condition of retaining the proper water level in all its members, and consequently is not subject to dangerous overheating by any single part becoming dry.

All boilers which I have constructed on this plan provide a good supply of steam with a moderate consumption of fuel. They are light, and easy to manage; and since they contain a large volume of water and steam, in proportion to their heating surface, they work with great regularity and security, and maintain the pressure, if ordinary care is used in the firing, with scarcely perceptible variation. They are, moreover, exceedingly easy to clean, for it will be found that the deposit generally collects against the end covers. I have seldom found any in the middle of the cylinders, and whatever there is may be easily removed with a scraper.

102. I now pass on to the description of my *feeding apparatus*. I endeavour to place this as near as possible to the boiler, so that the man who attends to the latter may have the feed apparatus constantly before his eyes, and be able conveniently to regulate it to the varying requirements of the water supply. The engine itself is, however, generally at some distance from the boiler; and I usually make its connection with the feed-pump outside the engine-room, and work the latter by an eccentric arrangement on the fly-shaft. Wherever possible, I avoid the common form of eccentric, as it is usually made for working the valves of both high and low-pressure engines: it requires much labour in the manufacture, and causes great friction in the working. I generally in lieu fix a flanch with an eccentric gudgeon at the end of the fly-wheel shaft, or else set a pin in a wheel geared into another on the shaft. The gudgeon works the connecting rod communicating with the pump. In most cases I find opportunity for putting the mechanism to move the pump-rod on the box or cistern in which the pump is placed, as shown in figs. 19 and 20. The before-mentioned connecting rod, of which only the end (*a*) is seen, moves the lever (*b*). This lever is provided

with a long slit in which a gudgeon (c) is screwed. The connecting rod (a) grasps this gudgeon by a notch, in the same manner as the eccentric rod of low-pressure engines (see fig. 21). By means of the slit in the lever (b), the gudgeon may be fixed nearer to or farther from the fulcrum, and the stroke of the pump thereby increased or diminished as required. The axle (d) moves in plummer blocks (e), fixed to the cistern, and carries the lever (f), which works the pump-rod (g). I case all the gudgeons, and line all the holes of these joints with steel, first forged and turned into form, and then hardened. All link joints in the engine itself I make in the same manner; for I have found it an indispensable precaution if they are to endure long and work easily. Such joints are useless made in brass; they soon wear and become loose, and then their destruction is inevitable. Soft iron is subject to the same objection, and moreover causes much friction. But hardened steel surfaces wear many years without requiring any repair, and do not get loose even if exposed to shaking or concussion. I strongly recommend this plan.[38]

I generally lengthen the lever (b) upwards, and provide it with a handle, whereby the pump may be worked when necessary by manual power, after the rod (a) (provided also with a handle) has been released from the gudgeon (c).

103. My feed-pumps are always piston-pumps, which I prefer to those with plungers. Practice has led me to the preference, and this must always be the Engineer's

[38] All good manufacturers in England adopt this method of making link joints. It is as old as Soho.—Tr.

surest guide. I do not venture to explain how the advantage arises; but experience often negatives the most cogent reasonings and the most scientific calculations, in a manner difficult to explain.

In fig. 23, my feed-pump and its cistern are shown in section. The pump consists of a gun-metal barrel (*a*), accurately bored and polished. At the bottom end is a side pipe (*b*) leading into the valve-box (*c*). Both parts are cast in one piece with the barrel. In the upper part of this box is the discharge-valve (*d*); and in the lower part (*e*) is the suction-valve (*f*). The valves have three-cornered stalks, the three sides being hollowed out to increase the water way, like the safety-valve. The stalk of the suction-valve has underneath, at *g*, a small cylindrical prolongation with a knob: under this lies, on the bottom of the cistern, a small lever (*i*), which, when moved upwards by the wire (*k*), presses against the knob, and opens the valve. By this the supply to the boiler from the pump is stopped, the water returning into the cistern. In order to keep the valve open, the upper end of the rod (*k*) is provided with a ball (*l*) which, when the rod is lifted, may be made to rest on a notch in the braket (*m*) (see fig. 25). I have used this simple arrangement for throwing the pump out of action for upwards of twenty years. It has the great advantage that but little power is required to effect the stoppage, a small force being sufficient to keep the valve open. This property is of especial value where a self-regulating feed is adopted, and when only a limited power is available to control the flow of water. The cocks commonly used for that purpose soon get out of order, and leak, besides forming a considerable addition to the apparatus, whereas my plan is simple and sure, and acts by the existing valve alone.

Another advantage of this arrangement is that it saves the power required to work the pump, while it is thrown out of action.[39] If the suction-pipe is stopped, a vacuum must, at every stroke, be formed under the piston, which not only consumes power, but tends to produce leakage.

In order to prevent the penetration of air into the pump, I use no suction-pipe, but place the whole under water, the top of the working barrel being 2 or 3 inches below the surface. Or if the height of the pump does not easily allow of this latter provision, I make a deep bell-shaped enlargement (fig. 22, a) to the top of the pump, which may contain enough water to exclude the air from the piston. If any leaks exist in the packing, the water will have a tendency to exude, from the great pressure in the down-stroke, and will keep the bell full. Any overflow falls by the pipe (b) back into the cistern. By these arrangements no air is allowed to come in contact with the pump, and I have found them perfectly effectual.

104. For feed water I always use fresh cold water, not the condensed water from the engine. The latter is indeed as good as distilled, and is less liable to cause deposit; but it carries much grease from the engine with it, acquiring thereby a milky, soapy condition. Now when such water mixes with the cold water in the cistern, the grease collects upon the pump and stops the valves, causing constant danger of derangement. Fresh cold feed water has indeed the disadvantage of requiring somewhat more heat to evaporate it, but the difference is very small in proportion

---

[39] It is peculiarly applicable to hydraulic presses.

to the whole heat required,[40] and not to be mentioned in opposition to the advantages gained from a regular and secure water supply. With regard to the greater risk of incrustation from fresh cold water, it is enough to remark that in high-pressure boilers this deposit is loose, and causes little inconvenience. When the waste steam is used to warm rooms, the condensed water may be led back into the feed cistern, taking care, however, that the greasy portion proceeding from the engine is not mixed with it. This may be easily prevented by making an enlargement in the exhaustion-pipe immediately beyond the engine, and carrying the greasy water away from this by a small tube.

If it is wished to warm the water before it enters the boiler, this may be best done in vessels interposed between the boiler and the pump; the external surfaces being heated either by the waste steam or the heat from the flues. These vessels then become parts of the boiler, and the water in them sustains the boiler pressure. If the water is heated in these to the boiling point, the greater part of the deposit will fall in them, and arrangements must be made for cleaning them. But under all circumstances the feed-pump must work in *cold* water.

105. The valves of the feed-pump I make as light as is consistent with the necessary strength and durability, especially the suction-valve, in order that it may open freely. The three-cornered stalks should leave a clear opening of at least one-fourth of the area of the pump barrel, and should not be too loose in their guides, lest dirt should enter and stick them fast. It is enough if they

---

[40] This is shown in the original by a calculation.—Tr.

are so free that the valve will fall by its own weight upon its seat. The edges of the stalk should not be too sharp, lest they wear away and become loose. The length should be about double the diameter. The conical face should be narrow; *i. e.* its width not above ⅛ the diameter of the valve, which is ample for the highest pressure, if the metal is not too weak. The angle of inclination of the faces to the axis should be 45 degrees. The ring-shaped space between the edge of the valve head and the sides of the valve-box is often made too small: it should not be less than the fourth part of the diameter of the top of the valve.

The suction-valve may be made somewhat smaller than the delivery - valve. The former may then be inserted into and withdrawn from its place through the opening of the latter, and even be ground into its seat in the same manner. This arrangement has many conveniences in the manufacture, since no loose seat is necessary for the lower valve; and it has the advantage that both valves may be removed and examined without disturbing the pump. I have found this advisable, and unattended with any disadvantage.

In small pumps, whose valves are most liable to derangement, it is to be recommended that the apparatus for lifting the suction-valve should be made strong, and so arranged that when lifted it may, if required, be caused to strike against the delivery-valve, and so raise both together. By this means a strong rush of water may be caused from the boiler to the cistern, by which both valves will generally be thoroughly cleaned, and any intervening substances removed.

The delivery or efflux-valve must have a stop-pin fixed over it, to prevent it from rising too high. This is shown in fig. 23, at *n*: *o* is part of the feed-pipe. Or sometimes I place instead a small cross bridge over the valve, or fix a cross piece upon the valve itself; either of these answering the same purpose.

In order to provide a hold upon the valve when it is necessary to grind it into its seat, I cut a nick in its half-round head, similar to that in a wood screw. In this a suitable tool is inserted when it is necessary to grind the valve.

106. I make the diameter of the pump small in proportion to its length of stroke. This has not only the advantage that the packing is tighter and more easily renewed, but the friction is less, and any air which may enter is sooner and more effectually expelled. In order also further to facilitate the expulsion of the air, I take the precaution of making the piston approach, when at the bottom of its stroke, as nearly as possible to the side opening at the bottom of the barrel; adding sometimes a protuberance on the under side of the piston, which descends beyond the edge of the opening, and so aids in expelling the air along the passage and through the delivery-valve, even when the stroke of the pump may be shortened.

107. The pump working in cold water, the packing of the piston may be made of leather. There is, however, the chance that if the delivery-valve leaks, the hot water from the boiler may find its way back, and injure this kind of packing. I have lately arranged leather packing successfully, by turning a groove in the piston so deep that the leather, when fixed in it, fills the cylinder to such an extent as to make a tight packing. The leather must

exactly fill the length as well as the breadth of the groove. The ends being cut into exact form, must abut together. This kind of packing is shown in figs. 26 and 27: the former represents the piston without, the latter with, the packing: *a*, fig. 26, is the groove; and *a*, fig. 27, shows the abutting joint of the packing. It will, if carefully made, become perfectly tight when wet. If the leather is held fast round the piston, the whole may be introduced into the pump barrel without difficulty, especially if the top of the latter is given a slight conical enlargement. The outer or smooth surface of the packing should be smeared with tallow. This packing will be very durable if the accident above alluded to does not occur. I have used one more than a year. It may be easily renewed when necessary.

If, however, it is feared that the leather may be destroyed by the access of scalding water, a packing may be made of gaskets of loose-spun hemp or flax, wrapped evenly and firmly round the piston, and afterwards steeped in melted tallow. Such a packing is tight and durable, although it will not last so long as leather. In order to make the gaskets hold more firmly on the piston, I roughen the groove in the manufacture by pecking it out all over with a sharp-pointed tool. The packing must never be less than $1\frac{1}{2}$ inch long, and as a general rule, the length should at least be equal to the diameter.

108. I have alluded to the possibility of the hot water returning from the boiler by a leaky state of the delivery-valve. This may also produce danger of the water level in the boiler sinking lower than is consistent with safety. Such an accident may be guarded against in two ways: either by making use of two delivery-valves, one over

the other, both of which the water may pass through successively; or by inserting the supply-pipe only 2 or 3 inches deep in the water of the boiler, so that after a little sinking, steam only may issue. The former plan is most to be recommended, since it is scarcely to be supposed that both valves will forsake their duty at one time. A watchful attendant will soon be aware of the derangement by the sinking of the water level in the boiler, the appearance of steam in the water cistern, and the heating of the feed-pipe; and he may then soon stop the mischief by shutting off the connection between the feed-pump and the boiler. For this purpose a cock should always be placed in the feed-pipe; a provision useful also when any slight attention is wanted to the pump: this may often then be given, and slight derangements remedied, without disturbing the action of the engine.

109. When water runs of itself into the feed cistern, or may be obtained from the pumps of the establishment, it may be kept at its proper height in the cistern by a float-cock, or a waste-pipe, as may be thought best. But if the water has to be raised, it is always better to do this by means of a separate pump than to make use of the suction-pipe of the feed-pump for the purpose. The additional cold water pump may then be a simple lifting pump, worked by the machinery of the feed-pump itself. It should raise somewhat more water than is required, and the surplus be allowed to flow back again by a waste-pipe. This overflow will then always serve as an index to show whether the supply goes on properly. Or if thought desirable, a float in the cistern may be made to sound a bell when the water is too low.

I formerly placed a strainer before the suction-pipe of the feed-pump; but this I found to interfere with the action of the apparatus for raising the suction-valve. It is better to make a frame of fine brass wove wire, 50 or 60 wires to the inch, and to place this in the cistern in such a manner as to divide it into two unequal parts : the water is delivered in the smaller of these, and the feed-pump stands in the larger. All the feed water must then pass the sieve and deposit its impurities before it reaches the pump. The frame may be fixed in a groove, and its edges made tight round the cistern by leather or felt. It may then easily be removed and cleaned. The larger division of the cistern will afford room for the float. The cistern must always be covered, to preserve it as much as possible from the entrance of dirt. It should have a draw-off cock, and should frequently be examined and cleaned; as should also the straining frame. This must be done more or less often, according to the state of the water used.

Soft river or lake water is much to be preferred to hard or spring water, whenever it can be obtained, as producing much less deposit in the boiler. It is liable, however, to be dirty after heavy rains; and in this case it should be collected in reservoirs, and the impurities allowed to subside before it is used.

If there is no vacuum-valve to the boiler, care must be taken to shut the cock in the feed-pipe whenever the engine is stopped, lest the boiler should fill itself with water through the feed-pump.

110. If preference is given to the plunger-pump for water feed, I recommend all the foregoing precautions

and rules to be followed as far as they will apply. It should be entirely sunk under water, and the opening leading from the plunger barrel to the delivery-valve should be immediately under the stuffing-box, in order that any air may escape. There should not be too much play round the plunger in the barrel, never exceeding one-sixth of the diameter of the former. The plunger should always be of copper or gun-metal. All the valves and other parts may be similar to those described above.

111. The *steam gauge* I use is a common manometer. The pipe leading from this to the boiler must always be provided with a stop-cock; otherwise, if a vacuum should be formed in the boiler, the air in the manometer tube may escape. Or as a greater precaution the boiler may be furnished with a vacuum-valve.[41] The steam should not be allowed to act immediately upon the mercury, as it would heat the instrument and affect its indication : this may be prevented by giving the tube a bend downwards before it reaches the manometer. Water will then collect and remain in this bend, and serve as a medium between the steam and the mercury, preserving the latter from the heat of the former. Care must be taken to make the steam-pipe open into the boiler as far away from the water as possible, otherwise there is a danger of its being stopped up with deposit.

[41] These valves, like safety-valves, require constantly to be looked to, or they will stick fast and become useless.

K

PRINTED BY W. HUGHES,
KING'S HEAD COURT, GOUGH SQUARE.

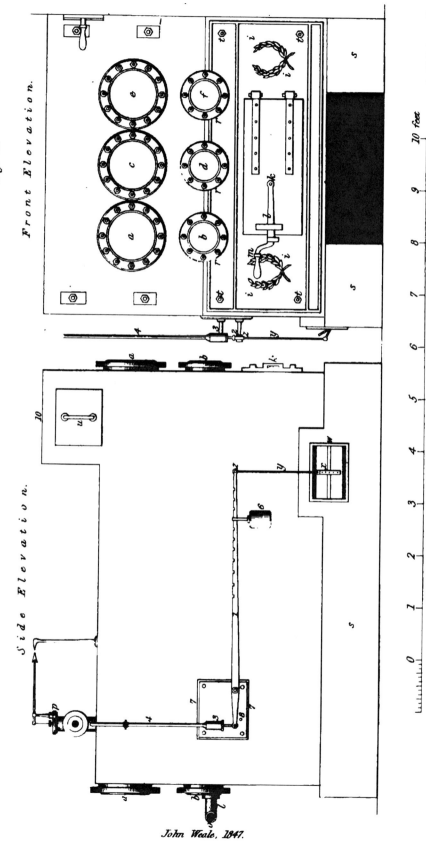

Pl. I.

Boiler for Small Engines.

Fig. 1.   Fig. 2.

Side Elevation.   Front Elevation.

0 1 2 3 4 5 6 7 8 9 10 feet

G. Gladwin. sculp.

John Weale, 1847.

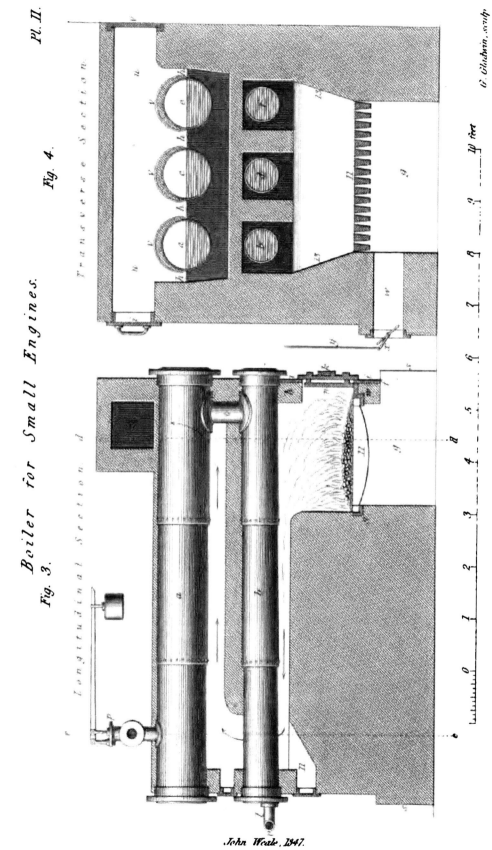

Boiler for Small Engines.

Pl. II.

Fig. 3.

Longitudinal Section d

Fig. 4.

Transverse Section

G. Gladwin. sculp.

John Weale, 1847.

Boiler for Small Engines.

Pl. III.

Fig. 5.

Transverse Section.

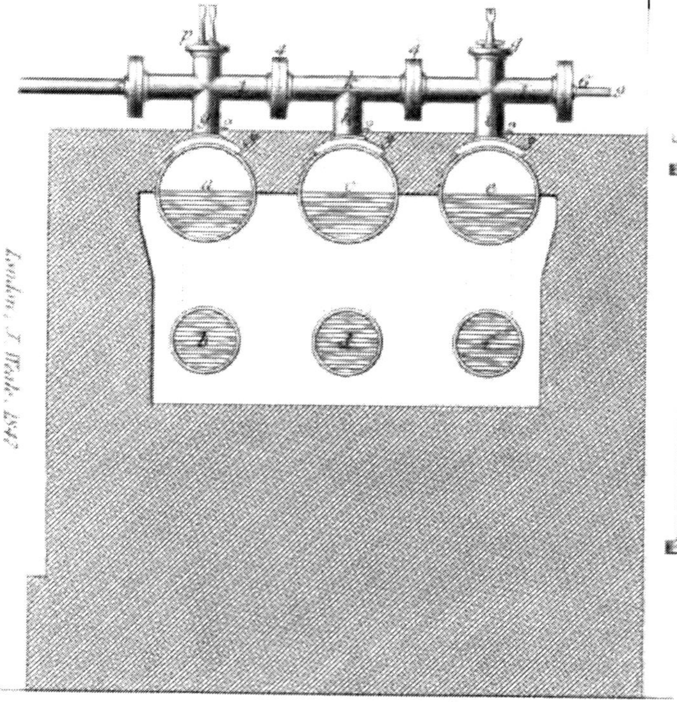

Fig. 6.

Horizontal Section.

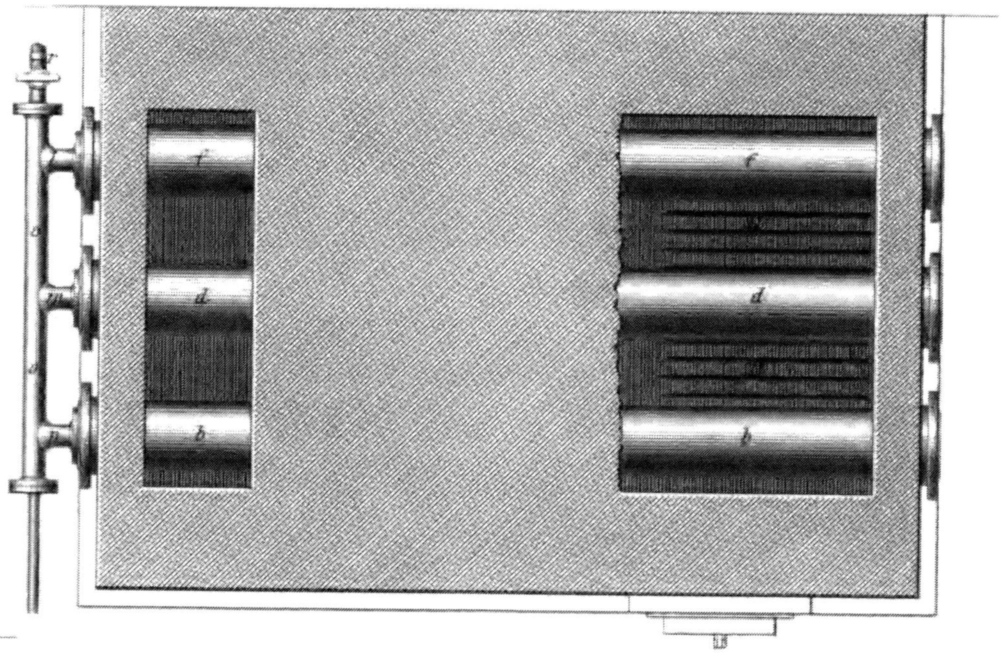

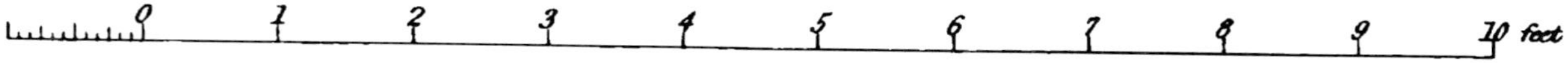
0 1 2 3 4 5 6 7 8 9 10 feet

London, J. Weale. 1847

G. Gladwin, Sculp.

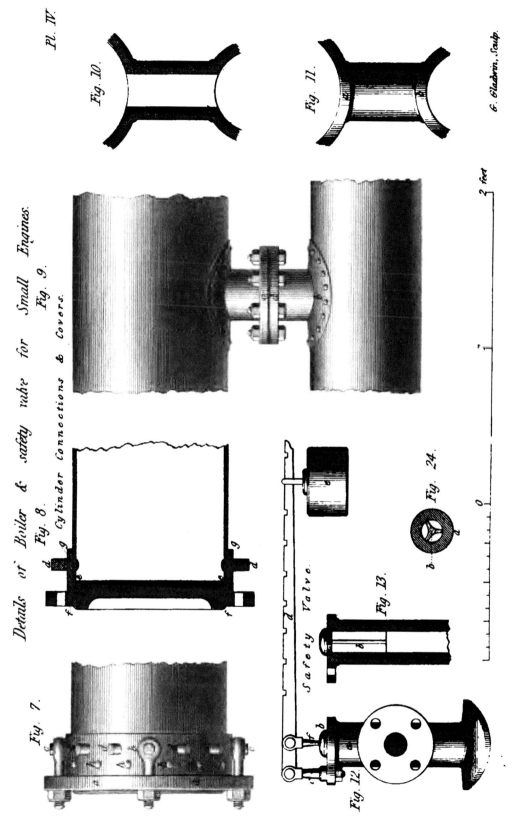

Pl. IV.

Details of Boiler & safety valve for Small Engines.

Fig. 7.

Fig. 8.

Cylinder Connections & Covers.

Fig. 9.

Fig. 10.

Fig. 11.

Safety Valve.

Fig. 12.

Fig. 13.

Fig. 24.

2 feet

G. Gladwin, Sculp.

London, J. Weale, 1847.

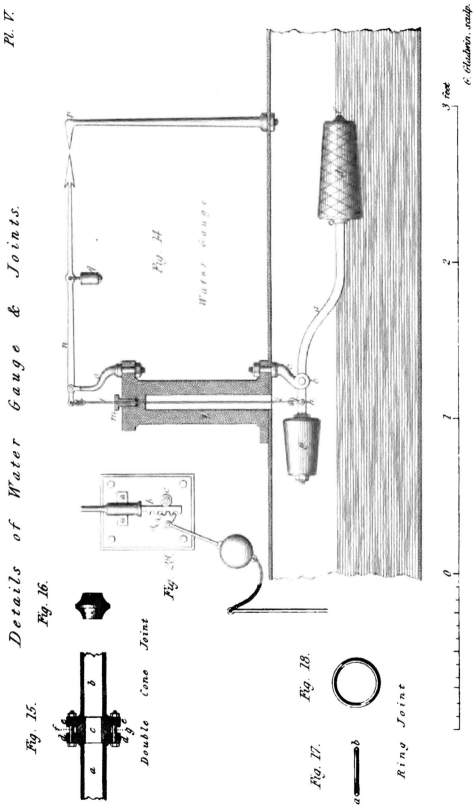

Pl. V.

Details of Water Gauge & Joints.

Fig. 16.

Fig. 15.

Double Cone Joint

Fig. 19.

Fig. 14.

Water Gauge

Fig. 18.

Fig. 17.

Ring Joint

3 feet

G. Gladwin. sculp.

John Wale. 1847.

Pl. V.

Details of Water Gauge & Joints.

Fig. 16.

Fig. 15.

Double Cone Joint

Fig. 14.

Water Gauge

Fig. 19.

Fig. 18.

Ring Joint

Fig. 17.

3 feet

G. Gladwin. sculp.

Mr. WEALE has recently published

THE ENGINEER'S AND CONTRACTOR'S POCKET BOOK

FOR THE YEARS 1847 AND 1848:

Remodelled and improved on Templeton's Engineer's Pocket Book.

CONTENTS.

THE ENGINEER'S AND CONTRACTOR'S POCKET-BOOK.

CONTENTS—*continued*.

Bound in roan, gilt leaves, Price 6s.

w/o
[illegible]
3

CPSIA information can be obtained at www.ICGtesting.com
Printed in the USA
241196LV00010B/66/P

9 781141 075928